POWER BASICS®

World Geography

Teacher's Guide

JWW693 v1.01

ISBN 978-0-8251-5673-1

J. Weston Walch, Publisher
P.O. Box 802 | Culver City, CA 90232
www.socialstudies.com/walch
Printed in the United States of America

Table of Contents

Power Basics®

Power Basics® Social Studies

Power Up Your Basic Skills Curriculum!

Learners are guided toward mastery of essential social studies content in U.S. history and government, geography, and world history. With extension activities, skills practice, and thorough reviews of concepts, this program invites all students to make the important connection between social studies and their own lives.

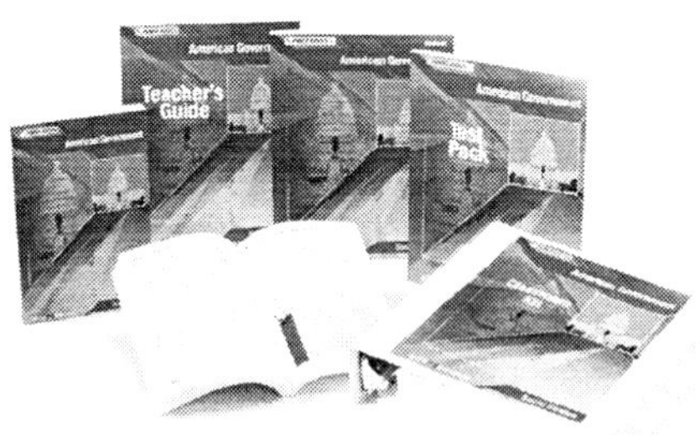

Power Basics on-level content and below-level readability pack a powerful punch!

Content adheres to the NCSS standards!

6 Programs!

Power Basics® American Government Second Edition

Power Basics® United States History Second Edition

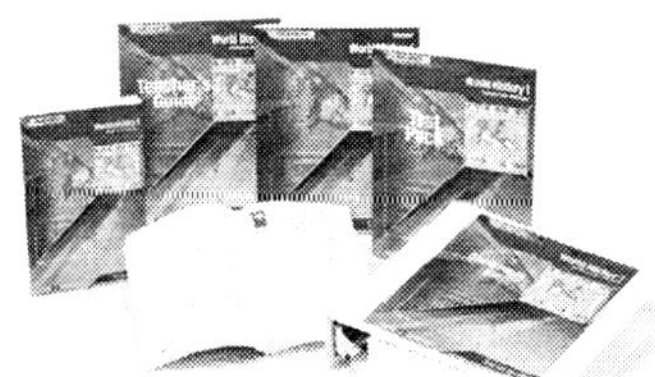

Power Basics® World History I Second Edition Prehistory to the Middle Ages

Power Basics® World Geography Second Edition

Power Basics® American Government Second Edition

Show students how the U.S. government works for them!

- Explains the organization of the U.S. government, from the local to national level
- Examines historical events that led to the development of U.S. democracy
- Covers all aspects of elections from candidate selection to the voting process
- Includes landmark court decisions that shaped the modern structure of the U.S. government

Power Basics® United States History Second Edition

Watch the U.S. grow from a small colony to a modern powerhouse!

- Examines U.S. history from the colonial period through the present
- Engages students with captivating profiles of key historical figures
- Covers the consequences of conflicts from the Civil War and WWII to the Gulf War and beyond

Power Basics® World Geography Second Edition

Travel the world without leaving the classroom!

- Provides an overview of world boundaries
- Helps students readily visualize other parts of the world with easy-to-read, detailed maps
- Explains how boundaries change as new nations are formed
- Gives students an appreciation for other cultures with in-depth country profiles

Power Basics® World History Second Edition

Help students experience history beyond U.S. borders!

- Provides a comprehensive overview of world history, from prehistoric civilizations to modern cultures
- Presents engaging profiles of international historical figures
- Focuses on essential people, places, and events that shaped the modern world

Volumes:

World History I—Prehistory to the Middle Ages
World History II—Renaissance to the late 1800s
World History III—1900 to 2004

Power Basics® World History II

Second Edition: Renaissance to the late 1800s

Power Basics® World History III Second Edition

1900 to 2004

World History II: Student Book

IN REAL LIFE

Have you ever heard of Columbus, Ohio? What about Columbus, Georgia? Or any of the other dozens of "Columbuses" in the United States? All are named for Christopher Columbus. That's also where the space shuttle Columbia got its name. And, a whole country in South America—Colombia—is named for him.

PRACTICE 6—"Indians," "America," and the "New World"

Circle the letter of the correct answer to each of the following questions.

1. Why are Native Americans called "Indians"?
   a. because they lived in the West Indies
   b. because that's what they called themselves
   c. because Columbus thought they lived in the Indies
   d. because each culture had their own name for themselves

2. Why were the Americas called the "New World"?
   a. because Columbus was from the New World
   b. because the Americas were a "new world" to Europeans
   c. because that's what Native Americans called their land
   d. because it was another name for the Indies

3. Who was "America" named after?
   a. Amerigo Vespucci, an Italian explorer
   b. the Indians
   c. Christopher Columbus
   d. the Vikings

Lessons guide students toward mastery of essential social studies content.

World History II: Workbook

NAME:

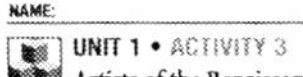

UNIT 1 • ACTIVITY 3
Artists of the Renaissance

One of the greatest features of the Italian Renaissance was the remarkable artwork that was produced. Many of the most famous paintings, statues, buildings, and pieces of literature were produced during the Italian Renaissance. In the exercise below you will use the information in your textbook to match the Renaissance artist with the great work of art associated with him.

Read the name of the artist or writer in the first column, and then fill in the second column with the artistic achievement that person is best known for. This will be a helpful study guide.

The first entry has been done for you.

Petrarch	Petrarch was a famous humanist writer whose greatest work was a collection of love poems known as the Book of Songs.
Boccaccio	
Giotto	
Donatello	
Raphael	
Michaelangelo	
Leonardo da Vinci	

Workbook pages provide activities featuring world history and cultures.

World History I: Workbook

NAME:

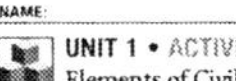

UNIT 1 • ACTIVITY 5
Elements of Civilization

The earliest civilization in Mesopotamia was Sumer. The Sumerians were the first to develop many new ideas and inventions. They lived very differently from the people of the Old Stone Age that we studied in the last chapter. To see how just how different the people of Sumer were compared to people of the Old Stone Age, complete the chart below. When you are finished, it will be easy to see how civilization changed the way people think and act.

You will be able to fill in almost all of the answers to the chart below from information found in your textbook. For some of the answers about Old Stone Age people you will have to use your imagination.

Characteristic	Old Stone Age People	People of Mesopotamia
How did people move objects from place to place?		
How did people communicate ideas to other people?		
What types of food did people eat?		
What type of government and laws did people have?		
What types of buildings did people live in?		
What types of work did people do?		

Workbook activities provide a thorough review of essential concepts.

CLASSROOM SET INCLUDES:
10 Student Books, 1 Student Book Teacher's Guide, 10 Workbooks, 1 Workbook answer key, 1 Test Pack

CLASSROOM KIT INCLUDES: (all reproducible)
1 Binder, 1 Student Book, 1 Student Book Teacher's Guide, 1 Workbook, 1 Workbook answer key, 1 Test Pack

To the Teacher

Overview

Power Basics® is a complete textbook program designed to meet the needs of students who are daunted by the length and complexity of traditional textbooks. The goal of all textbook programs is to provide students with important new information. However, in traditional textbook programs, this goal is often overshadowed by other considerations. Many textbooks are written for the above-average reader and cover a wide range of content. They are filled with photographs, illustrations, and other visual elements. For some students, the amount of material is overpowering, the visual elements are distracting, and the rapid pace is unnerving. In *Power Basics*®, we revisited the basic goal, developing a streamlined textbook program that presents the essential content students need to succeed.

Program Components

As with traditional textbook programs, *Power Basics*® includes a core textbook and ancillary products designed to round out the program. The student text provides coverage of the essential content in each subject area. A consumable workbook provides a variety of activities for each lesson, including practice activities, extension activities, and activities designed for different learning styles.

Teacher support materials include a teacher's guide and test pack for each student text. The teacher's guide includes the following: an overview of each unit in the student text; suggestions for extension activities; the student text glossary and appendix; a complete answer key to all practice activities and unit reviews in the student text; classroom record-keeping forms, and graphic organizers for student use.

For more detailed assessments, the test pack offers a pretest, unit tests for each unit in the student text, a posttest, and test-taking strategies for students.

Student Book Organization

The student text is divided into units. Each unit contains a series of lessons on related topics, with one lesson for each topic. Each lesson begins with a clear, student-centered goal and a list of key words that are introduced in the lesson. The definitions for these words are found in the glossary, located in both the student text and the teacher's guide.

Next comes a brief introduction to the topic of the lesson, followed by instructional text that presents essential information in short, easy-to-understand sections. Each section of instructional text is followed by a practice activity that lets students apply what they have just learned. A unit review is provided at the end of each unit to assess students' progress. The review is followed by one or more application activities that encourage students to extend and apply what they have learned.

The student text also includes several special features. "Think About It" sections ask students to use critical-thinking skills. "Tip" sections give students useful hints to help them remember specific pieces of information in the student text. "In Real Life" sections show students how the material they are learning connects to their own lives.

The reference section at the back of the student text includes an appendix, a glossary (with pronunciation guide) that includes all vocabulary in the Words to Know sections, and an index to help students locate information in the text.

Record-Keeping Forms

To make record-keeping easier, we have provided a reproducible class chart that you can use to track students' progress. Fill in your students' names, and make copies of the chart for each unit in the student text. Add lesson numbers, lesson titles, and practice numbers as needed. We have also provided a generic grading rubric for the application activities in the student text so that these activities may be assigned for credit, if you wish. You may customize the rubric by adding more grading criteria or adapting the criteria on the sheet to fit your needs.

We're pleased that you have chosen to Power Up your Basic Skills Curriculum with *Power Basics*®!

To the Teacher, *continued*

Guide to Icons

Teacher's Guide

Teaching Tip

Practical suggestions help you to engage students in the learning process.

Differentiation

Different approaches to the content gives all learners the opportunity to connect to the material.

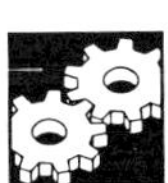

Thinking Skills

Helpful suggestions increase students' ability to think critically.

Fascinating Facts

These tidbits of information are guaranteed to pique your students' interest.

Student Text

Tip

Tips give helpful hints to boost understanding and retention.

Think About It

These sections develop critical thinking.

In Real Life

These features connect learning concepts to students' lives.

Workbook

Reinforcement

Reinforcement activities give students additional opportunities to practice what they have learned.

Multiple Intelligences

Different approaches capitalize on different learning styles and interests to help all students connect to the material.

Extension

Deepen and broaden learning with critical-thinking activities, real-life applications, and more.

Classroom Management

Student Name	Lesson No.: ______ Title: ______								
	Practice #___	Practice #___	Practice #___	Practice #___	Practice #___	Practice #___	Practice #___	Practice #___	Unit Review Score
1.									
2.									
3.									
4.									
5.									
6.									
7.									
8.									
9.									
10.									
11.									
12.									
13.									
14.									
15.									
16.									
17.									
18.									
19.									
20.									
21.									
22.									
23.									
24.									
25.									
26.									
27.									
28.									
29.									
30.									

Application Activity Rubric

Name ______________________________ Date ____________________

Unit __________ Activity ____

POINTS	4 all of the time	3 most of the time	2 some of the time	1 almost none of the time
followed directions				
organized material well				
used appropriate resources				
completed the entire activity				
showed an understanding of the content				
produced error-free materials				
drew logical conclusions				
where appropriate, listed sources used				

Use Chart

POWER BASICS WORKBOOK	STUDENT TEXT PRACTICE
Unit 1: Geography and Maps	
Activity 1: What Is Geography?	Practice 1: What Is Geography?
Activity 2: Types of Maps	Practice 2: Maps
Activity 3: Classroom Map	Practice 3: Getting Information from a Map
Activity 4: Continents and Oceans Game	Practice 4: Continents, Oceans, and Hemispheres
Activity 5: Latitude/Longitude	Practice 5: Latitude and Longitude
Activity 6: Create Your Own Island	Practice 5: Latitude and Longitude
Unit 2: The Americas	
Activity 7: Location: North America	Practice 6: Location
Activity 8: Population in North America	Practice 7: Population Distribution
Activity 9: Hawaii	Practice 8: Political Divisions of the United States
Activity 10: Nunavut	Practice 9: Political Divisions of Canada
Activity 11: Coastal Waters of North America	Practice 10: Islands, Coasts, and Bodies of Water
Activity 12: The Mississippi River	Practice 11: Inland Waterways
Activity 13: North American Landforms	Practice 12: Landforms
Activity 14: Introduction to Climographs	Practice 13: Climate
Activity 15: Agriculture: Wheat	Practice 14: Agriculture
Activity 16: Natural Resource Marketing Campaign	Practice 15: Natural Resources
Activity 17: Urban Centers: United States and Canada	Practice 16: Urban Centers
Activity 18: Location: Latin America	Practice 17: Location and Population Distribution
Activity 19: Population Distribution in Haiti	Practice 17: Location and Population Distribution
Activity 20: Political Divisions in Latin America	Practice 18: Political Divisions
Activity 21: Water in Latin America	Practice 19: Islands, Coasts, and Bodies of Water
Activity 22: The Amazon River	Practice 20: Inland Waterways
Activity 23: Latin American Landforms	Practice 21: Landforms
Activity 24: Climate Comparison	Practice 22: Climate and Agriculture
Activity 25: Food in the Americas	Practice 22: Climate and Agriculture
Activity 26: Urban Centers in Latin America	Practice 23: Natural Resources and Industry
Unit 3: Europe	
Activity 27: Population Density	Practice 24: Location and Population Distribution
Activity 28: Population Distribution in Hungary	Practice 24: Location and Population Distribution
Activity 29: Political Divisions in Europe	Practice 25: Political Divisions
Activity 30: Landforms of Europe	Practice 26: Peninsulas, Islands, and Bodies of Water
Activity 31: The Danube	Practice 27: Inland Waterways
Activity 32: The Winter Olympics	Practice 28: Landforms
Activity 33: Climate in Europe	Practice 29: Climate
Activity 34: Tulip History	Practice 30: Agriculture
Activity 35: Industry Comparisons	Practice 31: Natural Resources and Industry

Use Chart, *continued*

POWER BASICS WORKBOOK	STUDENT TEXT PRACTICE
Activity 36: The Berlin Wall	Practice 24: Location and Population Distribution
Unit 4: Africa	
Activity 37: Location: North Africa	Practice 32: Location
Activity 38: Population in Morocco	Practice 33: Population Distribution
Activity 39: Water in North Africa	Practice 34: Coasts and Bodies of Water
Activity 40: The Nile	Practice 33: Population Distribution
Activity 41: A Mystery Place in North Africa	Practice 35: Landforms
Activity 42: Climate of Fez	Practice 36: Climate
Activity 43: Farming in Dry Lands	Practice 37: Agriculture
Activity 44: Resources: North Africa	Practice 38: Natural Resources
Activity 45: Location: Sub-Saharan Africa	Practice 39: Location and Political Divisions
Activity 46: Comparative Urbanization	Practice 40: Population Distribution
Activity 47: Urbanization in Africa	Practice 40: Population Distribution
Activity 48: Around the Capes	Practice 41: Peninsulas, Capes, Islands, and Bodies of Water
Activity 49: Lake Victoria	Practice 41: Peninsulas, Capes, Islands, and Bodies of Water
Activity 50: The Congo River	Practice 42: Rivers
Activity 51: Landforms of Sub-Saharan Africa	Practice 43: Landforms
Activity 52: Climatic Differences	Practice 44: Climate
Activity 53: Diamonds	Practice 46: Natural Resources
Activity 54: Soccer by Another Name	Practice 46: Natural Resources
Unit 5: Russia, Central Asia, and the Middle East	
Activity 55: Location and Time Zones	Practice 47: Location
Activity 56: Russia and Uzbekistan	Practice 48: Population Distribution
Activity 57: The Trans-Siberian Railway	Practice 48: Population Distribution
Activity 58: Western Russia and Central Asia	Practice 50: Islands, Peninsulas, and Bodies of Water
Activity 59: The Volga	Practice 51: Inland Waterways
Activity 60: Landforms of Russia and Central Asia	Practice 52: Landforms
Activity 61: Climate in Moscow and Vladivostok	Practice 53: Climate
Activity 62: The Fertile Triangle: Ukraine	Practice 54: Agriculture
Activity 63: Natural Resources Game	Practice 55: Natural Resources
Activity 64: Local Government	Practice 56: Industrial and Urban Centers
Activity 65: Location: The Middle East	Practice 57: Location
Activity 66: Population: Israel and Saudi Arabia	Practice 58: Political Divisions and Population Distribution
Activity 67: Political Divisions in the Middle East	Practice 58: Political Divisions and Population Distribution

Use Chart, *continued*

POWER BASICS WORKBOOK	STUDENT TEXT PRACTICE
Activity 68: Global Chokepoints	Practice 59: Peninsulas, Islands, and Bodies of Water
Activity 69: The Euphrates	Practice 60: Inland Waterways
Activity 70: All Deserts Are Not Equal	Practice 61: Landforms
Activity 71: Baghdad's Climate	Practice 62: Climate
Activity 72: Irrigation	Practice 63: Agriculture
Activity 73: OPEC	Practice 64: Natural Resources and Industry
Unit 6: South Asia and East Asia	
Activity 74: Population in Dominoes	Practice 67: Population Distribution
Activity 75: Population: China and Bangladesh	Practice 67: Population Distribution
Activity 76: Political Divisions in Asia	Practice 66: Political Divisions
Activity 77: Archipelagos	Practice 68: Peninsulas, Islands, and Bodies of Water
Activity 78: The Yangtze River	Practice 69: Inland Waterways
Activity 79: Ring of Fire	Practice 70: Landforms
Activity 80: Climate in China	Practice 71: Climate
Activity 81: Rice	Practice 72: Agriculture
Activity 82: The Tokyo Fish Market	Practice 73: Natural Resources
Activity 83: Dams	Practice 74: Industry
Unit 7: Australia, Oceania, and Antarctica	
Activity 84: Location: Australia	Practice 75: Location
Activity 85: Population: New Zealand	Practice 77: Population Distribution
Activity 86: Water, Oceania, and Australia	Practice 78: Islands and Bodies of Water
Activity 87: The Murray River	Practice 79: Rivers and Lakes
Activity 88: A Mysterious Place in Australia	Practice 80: Landforms
Activity 89: Climate in Australia	Practice 81: Climate
Activity 90: A Country of Sheep	Practice 82: Agriculture
Activity 91: Thinking About Energy Sources	Practice 83: Natural Resources and Industry
Activity 92: Antarctica: Honoring Explorers	Practice 87: Landforms and Iceforms
Activity 93: Two Polar Expeditions	Practice 88: Climate
Activity 94: Climate in Antarctica	Practice 88: Climate

Unit 1: Geography and Maps

Unit 1 introduces the concept of geography as concerning both places and maps and the special terms and symbols used in geography. Lesson 1 is this unit's sole lesson. It opens with a discussion of the term *geography* and an explanation of maps, including the globe. Then Lesson 1 goes on to explore the types of information that maps can show, the features used in reading a map (compass rose, scale, and legend), the parts of a globe (continents, oceans, and hemispheres), and the globe's latitude and longitude lines. Students will use this basic information on geography and maps to explore the geography of various parts of the world in subsequent units of this book.

Lesson 1—Geography and Maps

Goal: To learn the special terms and symbols of geography and to use them to get and understand information from maps

WORDS TO KNOW

climate map
coast
compass rose
continents
degrees
due
elevation map
equator
globe
hemisphere
hydrographer
international date line
key
land use map
landforms
latitudes
legend
longitudes
maps
meridians
oceans
parallels
population
population map
prime meridian
product map
rainfall map
resources map
road map
scale
sphere

Notes on Application Activity in Student Text

Activity	Skills Applied	Product
Maps in Newspapers	gathering information, preparing a visual presentation	map

Additional Activity Suggestions

- Students can develop a dictionary of geographical terms as an ongoing project. For every lesson, have each student transcribe definitions of boldfaced terms such as *coast, peninsula,* and *cash crops.* Set up each student's dictionary in a loose-leaf notebook or card file. Or, have them create a computer database of terms. Encourage students to consult their dictionaries as they work through each lesson. Most terms, once introduced, are used several times throughout the course.

- To make map study more concrete, draw a large outline of a map on the floor with chalk or masking tape. (It does not have to represent a real location.) Add a compass rose showing only north. Have students orient themselves by using north to determine the other directions. Place classroom objects at various points around the map. Then have students stand on the map and tell which direction they would have to go to reach a particular object. ("Go north four steps. Turn toward the east. Take two steps to the east.")

Differentiation

- Each lesson in this book includes a map of the region discussed in that lesson. Some students may grasp a region's location in the world and in relation to other regions best by finding that region on a globe of the world. As you work through the lessons of this book, be sure to have a globe of the world available in the classroom. Students can go to the globe, locate the region under discussion on it, and point out the location to classmates. Using the globe can also help students confirm understanding of latitude, longitude, and hemisphere. Invite students to trace latitude and longitude lines halfway around the globe from where they live. Ask them what country lies halfway around the world from their home. In what hemisphere is that country? From looking at the globe, what might be the best way to travel from the students' home location to the foreign country?

Unit 2: The Americas

Unit 2 presents the geography of the Americas. Lesson 1 examines the geography of the United States and Canada, discussing the location of both countries on the North American continent. The lesson goes on to explore these neighboring nations' population distribution (and its relationship to climate and bodies of water), their political divisions, their various water resources and landforms (some shared), and their climates, agriculture, natural resources, and urban centers. Students' understanding of this lesson's geography is facilitated by maps, of the United States and Canada, of landforms, of climate, of land use, and of urban centers. Lesson 2 addresses the geography of Latin America, including Mexico, the Caribbean island nations, Central America, and South America. The lesson examines Latin America's population distribution as related to climate zones, its political divisions, its various water resources and landforms, its climate and agriculture in various climate zones, and its natural resources and industry. Students' understanding of this lesson's geography is facilitated by maps of Latin America, of landforms, and of climate.

Lesson 2—The United States and Canada

Goal: To understand the geography of the United States and Canada and how it affects population and economic patterns in both countries

WORDS TO KNOW

agriculture	island	region
bay	natural resources	sea level
belt	navigable	silt
channel	peninsula	state
climate	plains	strait
East Coast	plateaus	taiga
elevation	political divisions	tributaries
gulf	port	tundra
industrialized	prairie	urban
industries	province	waterway
inlet	ranges	West Coast

PLACES TO KNOW

Alaska Range
Appalachian Mountains
Atlantic seaboard
Bering Strait
Brooks Range
Canadian Prairie
Canadian Rockies
Canadian Shield
Cascade Range
Central Plains
Coast Mountains
Great Lakes
Great Lakes region
Great Plains
Gulf Coast region
Hudson Bay
Mississippi River
Mississippi River system
Pacific Coast Region
Rocky Mountains
Sierra Nevada
St. Lawrence Seaway

Lesson 3—Latin America

Goal: To understand the geography of Latin America and how it affects population and economic patterns in the region

WORDS TO KNOW

altitude
bauxite
capital
developing economy
estuary
export
highlands
landforms map
Latin America
puna
rain forest
tierra caliente
tierra fría
tierra templada

PLACES TO KNOW

Amazon River
Andes Mountains
Brazilian Highlands
Caribbean Sea
Central America
Galápagos Islands
Guiana Highlands
Gulf of Mexico
Llanos
Mexico
Orinoco River
Pampas
Panama Canal
Paraná River
Patagonian Plateau
Río de la Plata
Rio Grande
Sierra Madre
South America
West Indies
Yucatán Peninsula

Notes on Application Activities in Student Text

Activity	Skills Applied	Product
Advertising Your State	gathering information, evaluating information, thinking creatively, preparing a visual presentation	advertisement
What's in a Name?	gathering information	written description

Additional Activity Suggestions

- Have students study weather maps for different regions of the Americas. Help them interpret the maps. Then ask them to consider how the geography of an area affects its weather. Students can use the weather maps to compare and contrast the effects of geography in two different areas. If students have access to the Internet, they can view weather maps on the following sites:

  —*UM Weather* (http://cirrus.sprl.umich.edu/wxnet/maps.html) provides access to dozens of forecasts, maps, and satellite photos of the United States.

  —*Weather Underground* (http://wunderground.com/global/Region/A2/Temperature.html) links students to weather maps and forecasts for countries all over the world.

- Maps can be used to help students trace their family histories. Ask students to interview family members to learn more about their ancestral origins. Encourage them to learn as much as they can about the geography of these places. Use pushpins, flags, or sticky notes to locate each person's ancestral origins on a large map Then have each student give a short oral presentation about their ancestral origins. Ask them to explain whether their current habits and customs were influenced by those origins.

Thinking Skills

Explain that the United States, for most of its history, has shared peaceful borders with its neighbors to the north and south. Ask students to think about and discuss our relations with these neighbors. For example:

- How much do students know about our neighbors? How many of them can identify the capital of Canada?
- What would life in the United States be like if we were on unfriendly terms with our neighbors? How might such conflicts affect daily life?
- How does the current peaceful situation work to the advantage of all the countries involved?

Unit 3: Europe

Unit 3 presents the geography of Europe. Its single lesson, Lesson 4, discusses Europe's location and its division for geographical study into two regions—Western Europe and Eastern Europe. The lesson then goes on to examine the distribution of Europe's dense population (mostly along rivers and coasts), its regional political divisions, its many peninsulas and islands, its various water resources, its landforms, its mostly temperate climate, its varied agriculture, and its natural resources and industry, including the disparities of those between Western and Eastern Europe. Students' understanding of this lesson's geography is facilitated by maps of Europe, of landforms, and of climate.

Lesson 4—Europe

Goal: To understand the geography of Europe and how it affects population and economic patterns in the region

WORDS TO KNOW

arm
densely populated
euro
European Union (EU)
ocean current
seas
self-sufficient
Soviet bloc
Soviet Union
temperate
textiles
warm westerlies

PLACES TO KNOW

Adriatic Sea
Aegean Sea
Alpine nations
Alps
Apennines
Balkan Mountains
Balkan Peninsula
Baltic Sea
Baltic states
Black Sea
Bosporus
British Isles
Bucharest
Carpathian Mountains
Corsica
Crete
Cyclades
Danube River
Eastern Europe
English Channel
Euboea
Greece
Iberian Peninsula
Iceland
Ionian islands
Ionian Sea
Italian Peninsula
Kiev
Mediterranean nations
Mediterranean Sea
Minsk
North European Plain (or Lowland)
North Sea
Odessa
Peloponnese Peninsula

Prague	Sardinia	Strait of Gibraltar
Pyrenees	Scandinavia	Tyrrhenian Sea
Riga	Scandinavian Peninsula	Ural Mountains
Ruhr Valley	Sicily	Western Europe

Notes on Application Activity in Student Text

Activity	Skills Applied	Product
Merci Beaucoup!	exploring a different language, gathering information, evaluating information, thinking critically	foreign phrases or sentences

Additional Activity Suggestions

- Invite people who speak European languages to teach your class proper pronunciation for statements translated in the application activity, "Merci Beaucoup!" You could also invite them to discuss their experiences in European countries.

- Have students find a pen pal from Europe. If they have access to the Internet, they can find a pen pal on-line and communicate through e-mail. For their first letter or message, suggest that they develop a list of questions for their pen pal. Have them ask about the country's land and water features, population, climate, agriculture, industry, and urban areas. This is a great way for students to learn about other parts of the world.

Differentiation

- Playing a game of "Where Am I?" will encourage active learners to memorize geographic facts. First, ask each student to enter three clues on an index card. Each student's clues should refer to one country in Europe. A sample clue might be "This country shares a border with France." Once all the clues have been written, collect the cards and set up two teams. Have each team take a turn presenting clues to students on the other team. If that student identifies the place on an index card after only one clue, his or her team wins eight points. If a guess is correct after two clues, the team wins four points. If it takes all three clues to get a correct answer, the team wins two points. The first team to reach a certain number of points wins.

Unit 4: Africa

Unit 4 presents the geography of Africa. Lesson 5 opens with an overview of the African continent as a whole, including its location and ways in which its enormous size is manifested. Lesson 5 then turns to an examination of the geography of the five countries of North Africa, including its population distribution and density (as largely related to the region's water resources), bodies of water and their coastlines, landforms (dominated by the great Sahara Desert), the mostly very dry climate, agriculture and the scarcity of arable land, and natural resources. Students' understanding of this lesson's geography is facilitated by maps of the African continent, of North Africa, and of this region's landforms and climate. Lesson 6 examines the geography of sub-Saharan Africa, beginning with its location on the globe and its political divisions by region and as affected by colonial rule. The lesson goes on to discuss population distribution, bodies of water and associated land formations, rivers, landforms, climate regions, agriculture, and natural resources and mining industries. Students' understanding of this lesson's geography is facilitated by maps of sub-Saharan Africa, of landforms, and of climate.

Lesson 5—North Africa

Goal: To understand the geography of North Africa and how it affects economic and population patterns in the region

WORDS TO KNOW

arable	population density	staple
oases	sand dunes	tropics

PLACES TO KNOW

Algeria	Mediterranean Sea	Strait of Gibraltar
Atlas Mountains	Morocco	sub-Saharan Africa
Egypt	North Africa	Suez Canal
Libya	Sahara Desert	Tunisia

Lesson 6—Sub-Saharan Africa

Goal: To understand the geography of sub-Saharan Africa and how it affects economic and population patterns in the region

WORDS TO KNOW

cape
carat
cash crops
commercial farming
deforestation
desert fringe nations
fault
glacier
gum arabic
humus
mining
productivity
savanna
sub-Saharan Africa
subsistence farming
trench
unpredictable rainfall

PLACES TO KNOW

Angolan Plateau
Blue Nile
Cape of Good Hope
Congo River
Congo River basin
Drakensberg Mountains
Ethiopian Highlands
Great Rift Valley
Gulf of Guinea
Kalahari Desert
Katanga Plateau
Lake Chad
Lake Malawi (Nyasa)
Lake Tanganyika
Lake Victoria
Lake Volta
Mount Kenya
Mount Kilimanjaro
Mozambique Channel
Namib Desert
Niger River
Nile River
Sahel
Somali Peninsula
Tibesti Mountains
Victoria Falls
White Nile
Zambezi River

Notes on Application Activities in Student Text

Activity	Skills Applied	Product(s)
Travel Lure	gathering information, preparing a visual presentation	travel poster
River Trip	gathering information, applying information, thinking critically, preparing a visual presentation	answers, map

Additional Activity Suggestions

- There are many aspects of African life that students might like to know more about. Suggest that they read a general article about an African country they are interested in, then narrow their interest to one topic, such as a major religion, gold mining, birds of the rain forest, or nomadic peoples. Have them prepare a written report, then share what they learned with the class.
- If you have Internet access, International Voices (http://www.kirkwood.edu/esl/index.htm) is a web site that offers a collection of essays written by ESL students. This site, sponsored by Kirkwood Community College in Iowa, provides a great way for students to explore other regions in the world.
- Also visit National Geographic on-line (http://www.nationalgeographic.com). This site posts featured articles from each month's issue and a cumulative photo gallery. It also reports on current geography in the news, gives updates to world atlases, and offers links and interactive activities.

Differentiation

- Using a large and current political outline map of Africa on heavy paper or cardboard, create (or have students create) several jigsaw puzzles of the nations of Africa. Each nation should be labeled with its name. Disassemble the puzzles. Then divide students into teams who work to reassemble their puzzle. You could make this a timed contest, or simply let students work until their puzzle is completed.

Unit 5: Russia, Central Asia, and the Middle East

Unit 5 presents the geography of Russia, Central Asia, and the Middle East. Lesson 5 examines the geography of Russia and Central Asia, noting their location in both Europe and Asia and the vast size of Russia. This lesson then goes on to cover population distribution (and its size vs. density), political divisions, bodies of water and associated land formations, inland waterways, the great variety of landforms, climate, agriculture, natural resources, and industrial and urban centers. Students' understanding of this lesson's geography is facilitated by maps of Russia and Central Asia, of landforms, and of climate. Lesson 6 looks at the geography of the Middle East, explaining its location and the shifting definition of which countries are included in the term Middle East. This lesson then goes on to explore political divisions by region, population distribution and densities, peninsulas and islands, bodies of water and inland waterways, landforms, climate (mostly very dry), agriculture, and natural resources and industry (dominated by oil). Students' understanding of this lesson's geography is facilitated by maps of the Middle East, of landforms, and of climate.

Lesson 7—Russia and Central Asia

Goal: To understand the geography of Russia and Central Asia and how it affects population and economic patterns in the region

WORDS TO KNOW

Central Asian republics
Commonwealth of Independent States (CIS)
crop yield
drought
Fertile Triangle
hydroelectric power
irrigation
landlocked
permafrost
Russian Federation
semiarid
steppe
subarctic
Trans-Siberian Railroad

PLACES TO KNOW

Aral Sea
Arctic Ocean
Armenia
Asian Russia
Azerbaijan
Black Sea
Caspian Sea
Caucasus Mountains
Central Siberian Plateau
Communism Peak
Dnieper River
Don River
European Russia
Georgia
Irkutsk
Ismail Samani Peak
Kamchatka Peninsula
Kara Kum Desert

Kazakhstan
Kuril Islands
Kyrgyzstan
Lena River
Magnitogorsk
Moscow
Novosibirsk
Ob-Irtysh River
Russia
Sayan Mountains
Sea of Okhotsk
Siberia
St. Petersberg
Tajikistan
Tashkent
Tian Shan Mountains
Turkmenistan
Uzbekistan
Verkhoyansk Range
Volga River
West Siberian Plain
Yablonovy Range
Yenisey River

Lesson 8—The Middle East

Goal: To understand the geography of the Middle East and how it affects economic and population patterns in the region

WORDS TO KNOW

archipelago
embargo
Fertile Crescent
Middle East
Nile River basin
prevailing wind
Tigris-Euphrates system

PLACES TO KNOW

Anatolian Plateau
Arabian Peninsula
Arabian Sea
Bahrain
Cairo
Cyprus
Elburz Mountains
Euphrates River
Jordan River
Mount Ararat
Mount Damavand
Nile River
Persian Gulf
Plateau of Iran
Red Sea
Sinai Peninsula
Suez Canal
Tigris River
Turkey
Zagros Mountains

Notes on Application Activity in Student Text

Activity	Skills Applied	Products
In the News	gathering information, evaluating information, preparing a visual presentation, preparing a written presentation	list of issues in the news, map, paragraph

Additional Activity Suggestions

- The United States imports many products from Asia and the Middle East. Have students use the scale on a world map to figure out how far products from different countries must travel to get to their hometowns. Make a chart that lists the products and the distance. Before students use the scale, suggest that they make estimates. Then, as they get more accurate measurements, have them revise their estimates.

- Have students trace and cut out outline maps of Russia and the United States, being sure to use maps with the same scale. Then have students lay the U.S. map over the map of Russia for a visualization of how much larger Russia is than the United States.

- Ask students to calculate what time it is in various cities in Russia based on the time in your classroom when they are doing this activity. Remind students about the international date line. Is it a different day of the week in any of the Russian cities as well as a different time of day?

- Imported oil is critical to the U.S. economy. Have students create a chart showing the number of barrels of oil the U.S. imports from each nation outside the United States, ordered from most to least by region. What countries and regions supply the most oil to the United States? The least? What percentage of total U.S. oil consumption is supported by foreign imports?

Teaching Tips

- Some geographical place names may be challenging for students to pronounce just from seeing the name in print—for example, Kyrgystan and Verkhoyansk. Pronounce each Places to Know term aloud for students. For more unfamiliar and challenging place names, write a pronunciation guide on the board for students to refer to while reading and discussing.

- Encourage students to keep a word journal of unfamiliar terms. Have them include the following in the journal:

  1. place name
  2. pronunciation
  3. location
  4. mnemonic device to help them remember the place name

Unit 6: South Asia and East Asia

Unit 6 presents the geography of South Asia and East Asia. Its single lesson, Lesson 9, discusses the location of South Asia and East Asia and political divisions by region. The lesson then goes on to examine population distribution and density, peninsulas and islands, bodies of water and inland waterways, landforms, climate, agriculture (and its differences between South Asia and East Asia), natural resources, and industry. Students' understanding of this lesson's geography is facilitated by maps of South Asia and East Asia, of landforms, and of climate.

Lesson 9—South Asia and East Asia

Goal: To understand the geography of South Asia and East Asia and how it affects economic and population patterns in the region

WORDS TO KNOW

alluvial plain
autonomous region
copra
delta
erosion
fodder
foothills
hemp
isthmus
jute
monsoons
oil refining
plantations
subcontinent
tableland
terracing
terrain
38th parallel
tin
tsunami
typhoon
volcano

PLACES TO KNOW

Altai Mountains
Arabian Sea
Bay of Bengal
Beijing
Brahmaputra River
Celebes Sea
Chang River
China
Deccan Plateau
East China Sea
Eastern Ghats
Ganges River
Gobi Desert
Great Indian Desert
Guangzhou
Himalayas
Hindu Kush
Honshu
Huang River
Indian Ocean
Indian Peninsula
Indian Subcontinent
Indochina Peninsula
Indonesia
Indus River
Irrawaddy River
Japan
Java Sea
Kabul River
Karakoram Range

K2
Kunlun Mountains
Malay Peninsula
Maldives
Mekong River
Mongolia
Mongolian Plateau
Mount Everest
New Guinea
North Korea
Papua New Guinea
Philippine Sea
Philippines
Plains of Hindustan
Plateau of Tibet
Sea of Japan
Shanghai
Singapore
South China Sea
South Korea
Southeast Asia
Sri Lanka
Taiwan
Thar Desert
Tian Shan Mountains
Tibet
Western Ghats
Xi River
Yellow Sea

Notes on Application Activities in Student Text

Activity	Skills Applied	Product(s)
How Crowded Is Your Town?	gathering information, applying information, drawing conclusions	population density of town or city
Protecting Mount Everest	gathering information, critical thinking, preparing a written presentation	list, paragraph

Additional Activity Suggestions

- Kites are popular in Asia. Students can research kites and use what they learn to make a colorful bulletin board. Because kite flying is an international sport, there are web sites that offer information about the history of kites and even directions for making them.

- Students interested in sports might search the Internet or read encyclopedia entries and other reference materials to find out more about sports in South Asia and East Asia. Suggest that one source they could consult is an almanac with statistics about Olympic athletes from these areas. Baseball fans might go on-line to search for Japanese baseball.

- Ask students to create a class display of before-after-after images of the Asian areas affected by the devastating December 2004 tsunami. The first "after" images would show the extent of damage in various places right after the tsunami struck. The second "after" images, where available, would show recovery efforts and completed recovery. Interested students could create a graphic that explains visually and in words how an undersea volcano results in the formation of a tsunami and how that tsunami travels across the ocean until it impacts landforms.

Unit 7: Australia, Oceania, and Antarctica

Unit 7 presents the geography of Australia, Oceania, and Antarctica. Lesson 10 examines the geography of Australia and Oceania, noting the location of Australia and of Oceania and its three groups of islands scattered across the Pacific. This lesson then goes on to discuss the varying types of political divisions of Australia and Oceania, the uneven population distribution, islands and bodies of water, rivers and lakes, landforms, climate, agriculture, and natural resources and industry. Students' understanding of this lesson's geography is facilitated by maps of Australia and Oceania, of landforms, and of climate. Lesson 11 covers the geography of Antarctica, noting its location and some facts that make this a continent of extremes. This lesson then goes on to discuss Antarctica's divisions and varying population, peninsulas and islands, bodies of water, landforms and ice forms, the extremely cold polar climate, and natural resources. Students' understanding of this lesson's geography is facilitated by maps of Antarctica and of its landforms.

Lesson 10—Australia and Oceania

Goal: To understand the geography of Australia and Oceania and how it affects economic and population patterns in the region

WORDS TO KNOW

Aboriginals
atoll
bight
coral reef
dependency
fiord
high islands
low islands
Oceania
reservoir

PLACES TO KNOW

Adelaide
Australia
Australian Alps
Australian Capital Territory
Ayers Rock
Bass Strait
Brisbane
Canberra
Cape York Peninsula
Central Lowlands
Coral Sea
Darling River
Eastern Highlands
Gibson Desert
Great Australian Bight
Great Barrier Reef
Great Dividing Range
Great Sandy Desert
Great Victoria Desert
Gulf of Carpentaria
Hawaii
Lake Eyre
Mauna Loa
Melanesia
Melbourne
Micronesia
Milford Sound
Mount Kosciusko
Murray River
New Guinea
New South Wales
North Island
Northern Territory

Nullarbor Plain
Perth
Polynesia
Queensland
Simpson Desert
Snowy Mountains
South Australia
South Island
Sutherland Falls
Sydney
Tasman Sea
Tasmania
Timor Sea
Torres Strait
Uluru
Victoria
Western Australia
Western Plateau

Lesson 11—Antarctica

Goal: To understand the unique geography of Antarctica

WORDS TO KNOW

Antarctic Treaty
Atlantic Convergence
blizzard
calving
cyclone
dry valley
ice floes
ice shelf
iceberg
pack ice
polar desert
precipitation
sea ice
south magnetic pole

PLACES TO KNOW

Alexander Island
Antarctic Circle
Antarctic Ocean
Antarctic Peninsula
Antarctica
Beardmore Glacier
Deception Island
East (Greater) Antarctica
Ellsworth Mountains
Filchner Ice Shelf
Lambert Glacier
Mount Erebus
Rockefeller Plateau
Ronne Ice Shelf
Ross Ice Shelf
Ross Island
Ross Sea
South Orkney Islands
South Polar Plateau
South Pole
South Shetland Islands
Southern Ocean
Transantarctic Mountains
Vinson Massif
Weddell Sea
West (Lesser) Antarctica

Notes on Application Activity in Student Text

Activity	Skills Applied	Products
Island or Continent?	gathering information, applying information, thinking critically	definitions, paragraph

Additional Activity Suggestions

- Students might do further research on volcanic activity. Suggest that they research the Ring of Fire and locate active volcanoes on a map. Have them think about and discuss ways that living near active volcanoes might affect daily life.
- The islands of Oceania were populated, over centuries, by people originating in South and East Asia. These people traveled thousands of miles over the open ocean in oceangoing canoes with sails. They had no modern navigational tools like the ones European explorers used to finally sail across the Atlantic and discover the "New World." Instead, the pioneers of Oceania relied on their knowledge and observations of the natural ocean environment. Ask interested students to research and report on just how these ocean sailors navigated their way across the Pacific Ocean.
- Have students imagine that they operate a touring business that brings tourists to Antarctica. Ask them to create a brochure advertising these Antarctic tours, designed to convince potential customers to sign on. The brochure should emphasize Antarctica's unique features, its challenging yet survivable climate, attractions for tourists, popular tourist activities, and travel mode and accommodations.
- Alternatively, students could select an island or island country/territory group of Oceania to promote. Students imagine themselves as officials of the government tourist department designing promotional materials to encourage tourists to visit.
- The race to be the first person to reach the South Pole was dramatic and, in part, tragic. Both Roald Amundsen and Robert Scott battled to reach the Pole in the early 1900s, just weeks apart. Have students report on this dramatic event, which enthralled Europe, perhaps using newspaper reports of the time or writing their own news reports. Students should also trace the routes and progress of the two expeditions on a map of Antarctica.

Fascinating Facts

- The kiwi is a bird that exists only in New Zealand. It is odd-looking, with a small head, a long and narrow bill, tiny wings, and no visible tail. It cannot fly. New Zealanders are very fond of their native bird. The kiwi is the national emblem of New Zealand and appears on the country's stamps, coins, and paper money. New Zealanders even refer to themselves as "kiwis."

Answer Key

Unit 1: Geography and Maps

Lesson 1: Geography and Maps

Practice 1: What Is Geography?

1. maps
2. globe
3. geography

Practice 2: Maps

1. land use
2. product
3. climate
4. population
5. road
6. rainfall
7. resources
8. elevation

Practice 3: Getting Information from a Map

1. b
2. a
3. c
4. c
5. a

Practice 4: Continents, Oceans, and Hemispheres

1. b
2. c
3. b

Think About It, page 12

Answers will vary, depending on where students live. If students live in the United States or Canada, they live on the continent of North America. Everyone living in North America lives in the Northern and Western hemispheres.

Practice 5: Latitude and Longitude

1. b
2. a
3. a

Unit 1 Review

1. b
2. d
3. c
4. c
5. a
6. a

Unit 2: The Americas

Lesson 2: The United States and Canada

Think About It, page 21

Answers will vary. Northern Canada is far north of the equator. Students should infer from this that northern Canada is very, very cold.

Practice 6: Location

1. F
2. T
3. T
4. F

Practice 7: Population Distribution

1. F
2. T
3. F
4. T

Practice 8: Political Divisions of the United States

The following states should be crossed out:

1. Michigan
2. Illinois
3. New York
4. Wyoming

Practice 9: Political Divisions of Canada

1. d
2. c
3. e
4. b
5. a

Practice 10: Islands, Coasts, and Bodies of Water

1. c
2. b
3. d
4. a

Think About It, page 29

Answers will vary. Water routes are one efficient way to transport goods and people. Both the St. Lawrence Seaway and the Mississippi River system provide vast networks of water routes. These networks enable towns along their banks to trade, prosper, and grow.

Practice 11: Inland Waterways

1. F
2. T
3. T

Practice 12: Landforms

1. b
2. c
3. b
4. c

Practice 13: Climate

1. F
2. T
3. T

Practice 14: Agriculture

1. b
2. c

Practice 15: Natural Resources

1. c
2. b
3. a

Practice 16: Urban Centers

1. d
2. b
3. a
4. e
5. c

Lesson 3: Latin America

Practice 17: Location and Population Distribution

1. T
2. F
3. T

Practice 18: Political Divisions

1. SA
2. C
3. M/CA
4. C

Practice 19: Islands, Coasts, and Bodies of Water

1. Pacific Ocean
2. Gulf of Mexico
3. Caribbean Sea
4. Atlantic Ocean
5. Panama Canal

Practice 20: Inland Waterways

1. c
2. b
3. c

Practice 21: Landforms

1. c
2. d
3. a
4. b

Practice 22: Climate and Agriculture

1. F
2. T
3. T
4. T

Practice 23: Natural Resources and Industry

1. c
2. b

Unit 2 Review

1. d
2. d
3. c
4. a
5. d
6. c
7. b
8. b
9. d
10. a
11. d
12. c
13. d

Unit 2 Application Activity 2

United States of America—accidentally named for explorer Amerigo Vespucci by a mapmaker who thought Vespucci had discovered the Americas

Costa Rica—named "rich coast" by Spanish explorers who found gold there

Honduras—name means "depths"; named by Christopher Columbus for deep waters off the north coast

Colombia—named after Christopher Columbus

Mexico—named after the Mexica, the original inhabitants of the area

Bolivia—named after Simón Bolívar, the man who led several South American countries to independence

Unit 3: Europe

Lesson 4: Europe

Practice 24: Location and Population Distribution

1. T
2. F
3. F
4. T

Practice 25: Political Divisions

1. c
2. b
3. g
4. a
5. h
6. e
7. d
8. f

Think About It, page 69

The Adriatic Sea has much warmer waters. The Adriatic Sea is located closer to the equator. This puts it in a warmer region than the Baltic Sea.

Practice 26: Peninsulas, Islands, and Bodies of Water

1. F
2. T
3. F
4. F
5. T
6. F
7. T

Think About It, page 70

Answers will vary.

Practice 27: Inland Waterways

1. c
2. b

Practice 28: Landforms

1. c
2. d
3. a
4. a

Practice 29: Climate

1. F
2. T
3. T
4. F
5. T

Practice 30: Agriculture

1. b
2. b
3. d
4. a
5. c

Think About It, page 80

Answers will vary.

Practice 31: Natural Resources and Industry

1. b
2. d
3. b
4. c

Unit 3 Review

1. b
2. d
3. c
4. a
5. d
6. a
7. b
8. d
9. c
10. a
11. a
12. d
13. c
14. a
15. b
16. b

Unit 4: Africa

Lesson 5: North Africa

Practice 32: Location

1. F
2. T
3. F
4. T
5. F

Practice 33: Population Distribution

1. d
2. d
3. a

Practice 34: Coasts and Bodies of Water

The following statements should be checked: 1, 3, 4

Practice 35: Landforms

1. a
2. c
3. b

Practice 36: Climate

1. T
2. T
3. F
4. T

Think About It, page 98

Answers will vary. Deserts can spread when there are droughts in the surrounding regions. Winds may blow sand from the desert onto nearby land. To stop a desert from spreading, countries can use plants and good farming methods.

Practice 37: Agriculture

1. c
2. b
3. d

Practice 38: Natural Resources

1. c
2. d
3. a

Think About It, page 100

Answers will vary. Oil exports are good for the economy. But water is essential for life. Also, many industries use water. If the profits from exporting oil could be used to pay for a reliable water supply, then the choice would be easy.

Lesson 6: Sub-Saharan Africa

Practice 39: Location and Political Divisions

1. c
2. c
3. d

Practice 40: Population Distribution

1. a
2. c
3. c
4. d

Think About It, page 107

Answers will vary.

Think About It, page 109

Answers will vary. It is important for landlocked countries to be on peaceful terms with their neighbors. A landlocked country may be dependent on its neighbors to reach the sea, or shipments may come by sea for the landlocked country. The landlocked country must rely on its neighbor to allow these shipments through.

Practice 41: Peninsulas, Capes, Islands, and Bodies of Water

1. d
2. e
3. b
4. c
5. a

Practice 42: Rivers

1. T
2. F
3. F
4. F

Practice 43: Landforms

1. c
2. d
3. d
4. a

Practice 44: Climate

1. F
2. F
3. T

Practice 45: Agriculture

1. T
2. T
3. T
4. T
5. T
6. T

Practice 46: Natural Resources

1. T
2. F
3. T

Unit 4 Review

1. d
2. c
3. b
4. d
5. a
6. b
7. d
8. d
9. a
10. c
11. b
12. b
13. a
14. d
15. b
16. a

Unit 5: Russia, Central Asia, and the Middle East

Lesson 7: Russia and Central Asia

Practice 47: Location

1. F
2. T
3. F
4. T

Practice 48: Population Distribution

The following statements should be checked: 2, 4

Practice 49: Political Divisions

The following statements should be checked: 1, 5

Practice 50: Islands, Peninsulas, and Bodies of Water

1. T
2. T
3. F
4. F
5. F

Practice 51: Inland Waterways

1. T
2. T
3. T
4. F

Practice 52: Landforms

1. b
2. b
3. d

Practice 53: Climate

1. T
2. F
3. T
4. T
5. F

Practice 54: Agriculture

1. c
2. a
3. c

Practice 55: Natural Resources

1. T
2. T
3. F

Practice 56: Industrial and Urban Centers

1. d
2. a

Lesson 8: The Middle East

Practice 57: Location

1. F
2. F
3. F
4. T
5. T
6. T

Practice 58: Political Divisions and Population Distribution

1. d
2. a
3. b

Practice 59: Peninsulas, Islands, and Bodies of Water

1. d
2. b
3. a
4. c

Think About It, page 147

Answers will vary. Two of the Middle East's greatest rivers—the Tigris and the Euphrates—run through central Iraq. Much of central Iraq lies between these two rivers.

Practice 60: Inland Waterways

1. T
2. T
3. T

Practice 61: Landforms

1. c
2. b
3. a

Practice 62: Climate

1. F
2. T
3. T

Practice 63: Agriculture

1. T
2. F
3. T
4. F

Practice 64: Natural Resources and Industry

1. c
2. c
3. a

Unit 5 Review

1. b
2. b
3. a
4. c
5. d
6. c
7. b
8. a
9. a
10. d
11. b
12. d
13. c
14. d
15. a
16. a
17. b

Unit 6: South Asia and East Asia

Lesson 9: South Asia and East Asia

Practice 65: Location

1. F
2. T
3. T
4. F

Practice 66: Political Divisions

1. d
2. b
3. f
4. a
5. c
6. e

Practice 67: Population Distribution

1. F
2. T
3. T
4. T
5. F
6. T

Think About It, page 171

Answers will vary. Like many other Western powers, France established colonies around the world in the 1800s. Vietnam, Laos, and Cambodia were part of the French empire from the late 1800s to the late 1940s. Throughout this period, French was taught in schools and used in government.

Practice 68: Peninsulas, Islands, and Bodies of Water

1. a
2. e
3. d
4. f
5. b
6. c

Practice 69: Inland Waterways

1. c
2. e
3. a
4. d
5. b

Think About It, page 175

Answers will vary.

Practice 70: Landforms

1. a
2. b
3. c
4. d
5. b
6. a

Practice 71: Climate

The following should be checked: 2, 3, 5

Think About It, page 183

Answers will vary. Students might consider how arable the land in each place is. They might also be concerned about climate. How much rain does each place get? Other concerns could be the potential for erosion and flooding. Also, students might want to know how close each farm is to a river for transportation purposes. They might also think about what crops they could grow in each place.

Practice 72: Agriculture

1. d
2. c
3. b

Practice 73: Natural Resources

1. a, b
2. a
3. b
4. a, b, d
5. d

Practice 74: Industry

1. T
2. T
3. F
4. F

Unit 6 Review

1. c
2. c
3. a
4. b
5. b
6. b
7. b
8. a
9. d
10. d
11. c
12. c

Unit 7: Australia, Oceania, and Antarctica

Lesson 10: Australia and Oceania

Practice 75: Location

1. F
2. T
3. T
4. F

Practice 76: Political Divisions

1. c
2. a
3. b

Practice 77: Population Distribution

1. T
2. F
3. T
4. F

Practice 78: Islands and Bodies of Water

1. c
2. a
3. d
4. b

Practice 79: Rivers and Lakes

1. F
2. T

Think About It, page 204

Answers will vary.

Practice 80: Landforms

1. b
2. c
3. a

Practice 81: Climate

1. T
2. F
3. F

Practice 82: Agriculture

1. a
2. c

Practice 83: Natural Resources and Industry

1. F
2. T
3. T

Lesson 11: Antarctica

Practice 84: Location

1. T
2. F
3. T
4. F

Practice 85: Divisions and Population

1. F
2. T

Practice 86: Peninsulas, Islands, and Bodies of Water

1. c
2. b
3. a

Practice 87: Landforms and Ice Forms

1. F
2. T
3. T
4. T
5. F

Practice 88: Climate

1. b
2. c
3. d

Practice 89: Natural Resources

1. T
2. F

Unit 7 Review

1. c
2. a
3. d
4. c
5. b
6. a
7. d
8. b
9. c
10. b
11. b
12. c
13. a
14. d
15. a

Graphic Organizers

Graphic organizers are useful tools for any learner. They ask students to apply critical-thinking skills to create or complete a visual representation of information. Graphic organizers require that students read, write, and think, which engages them thoroughly in the learning process.

Graphic organizers appeal to different learning styles. Visual, verbal/linguistic, mathematical/ spatial, and kinesthetic learners benefit by mentally and physically arranging and writing the material in the graphic organizer. Musical/rhythmic learners shine at finding and demonstrating patterns and relationships among different pieces of information. Intrapersonal learners think about their own learning process and reasoning when evaluating and categorizing information. And interpersonal learners gain insight by discussing their graphic organizers with others.

Graphic organizers help students see, organize, and evaluate their thinking, as well as information. Charts, tables, webs, maps, and other visual representations help cement students' knowledge. They are excellent planning and reviewing tools, and they provide a window into students' thought processes. For struggling students, graphic organizers are a convenient, compact way to store and review lots of information at once.

Information Web

Information gained from reading can be mapped in a web. Physically arranging and writing geographic material in a web helps students see the important features of a country or region by category. The web provides students with a graphically arranged set of lists that are easy to study and remember. Students can add or subtract information circles and lines as needed.

Venn Diagram

The Venn diagram will help students compare the similarities and differences between two different countries or regions. Students could choose to compare, for example, a West European country with a country of Eastern Europe. Or they could compare an arid nation with a well-watered nation, or an industrialized nation with a non-industrialized nation. The choices are myriad. When completed, the Venn diagram provides a clear review of the comparisons.

Comparison Matrix

The comparison matrix is another way for students to compare two countries or regions by geographical feature. Students could use completed information webs for each country or region to fill in the comparison matrix information. Again, the completed chart helps cement students' knowledge of the geography of the selected areas and provides an excellent reviewing tool.

Information Web

Write your country or region in the center circle. Then label each smaller circle with a feature of that country or region such as "location," "political divisions," "population," "bodies of water and waterways," "landforms," "climate types," "agricultural products," and "natural resources." Write details about each of these features within each smaller circle.

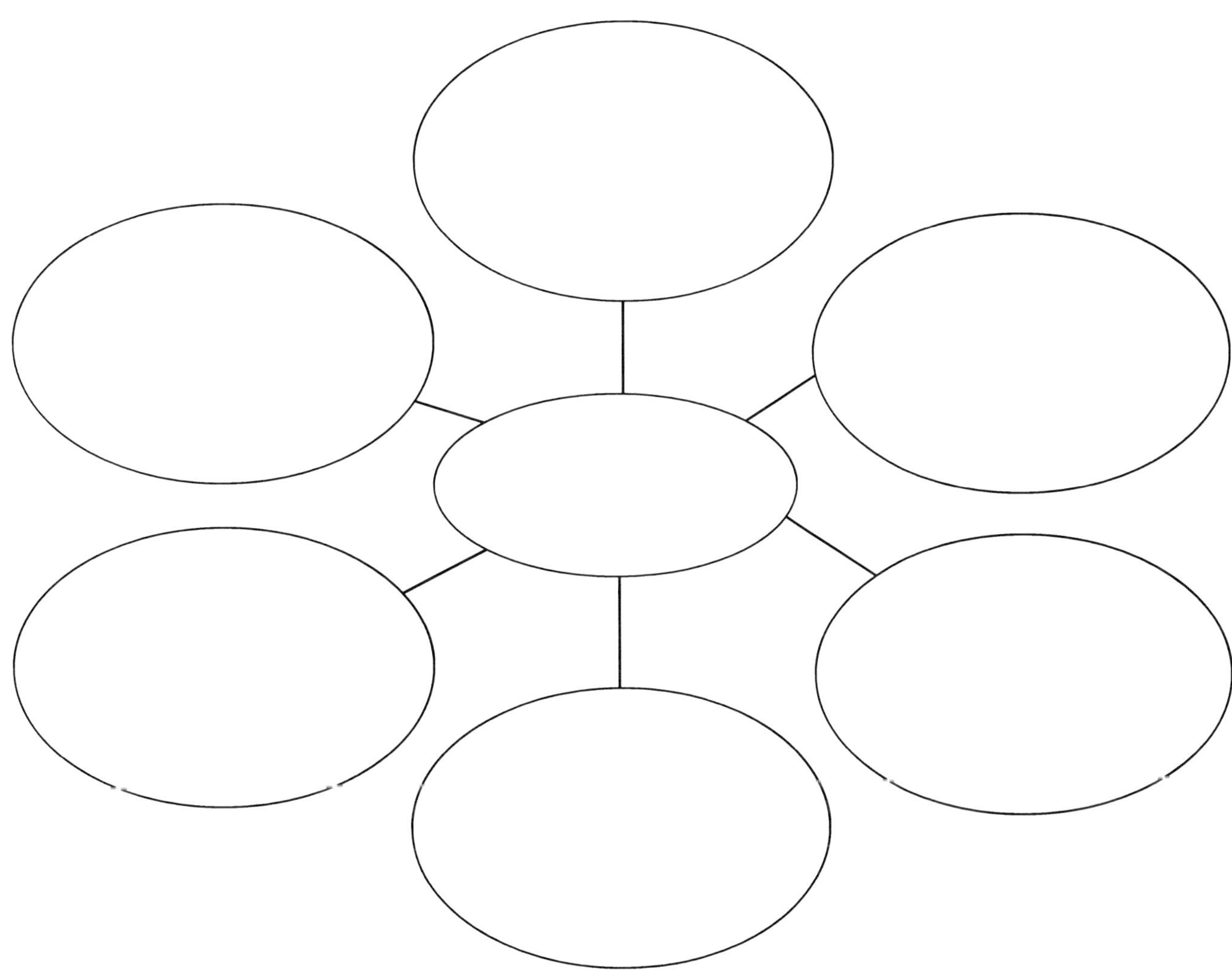

Venn Diagram

Complete the Venn diagram below with information about the ways that two countries of your choice are different—and alike. Write similarities in the area where the circles intersect. Write differences in the areas where the circles don't intersect. Don't forget to label both circles.

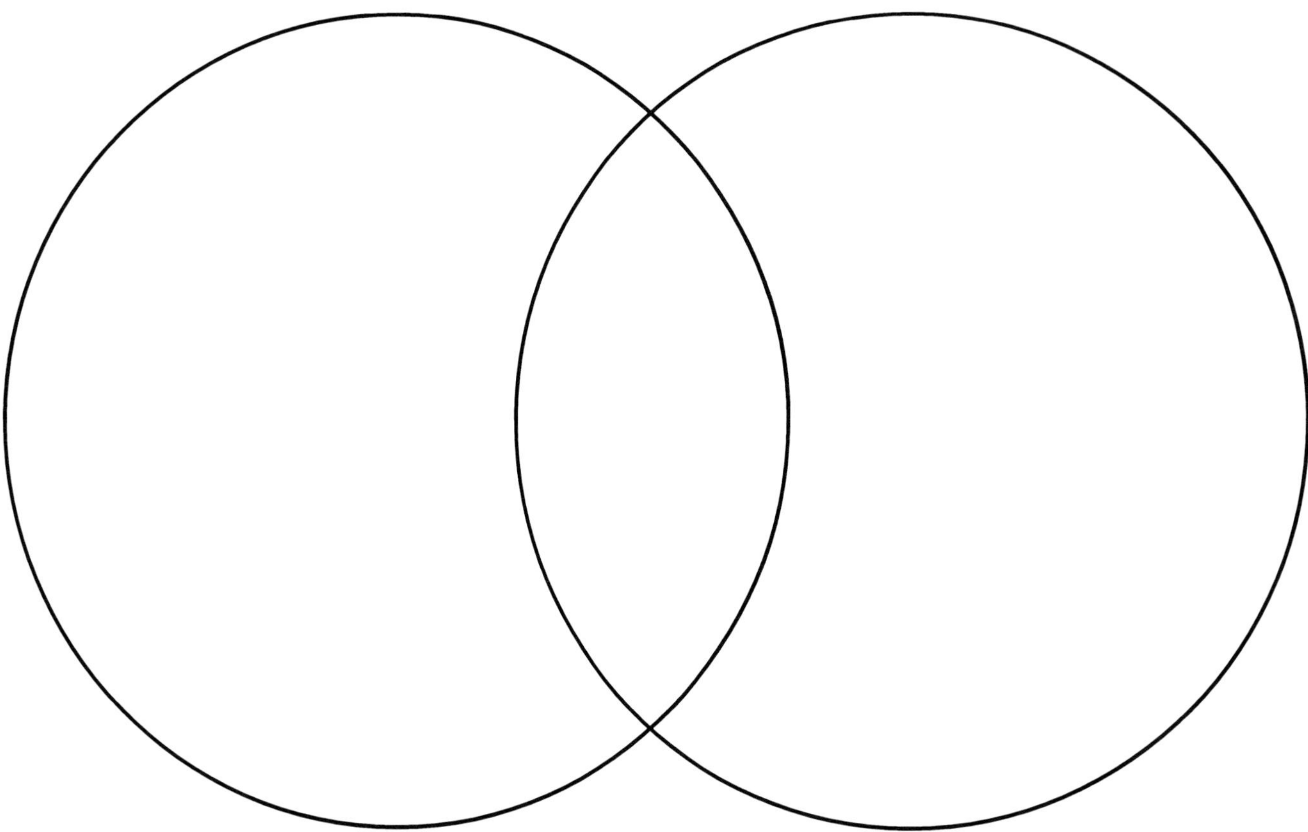

Comparison Matrix

Write the country or region you are comparing at the top of each column. Write one feature at the start of each row, such as "location," "political divisions," "population," "bodies of water and waterways," "landforms," "climate types," "agricultural products," and "natural resources." Add or delete rows and columns as needed. Then fill in each box in the matrix with the relevant information.

	Country/Region	Country/Region
Feature		
Feature		
Feature		
Feature		
Feature		

Student Book Appendix

PLACES TO KNOW

Adelaide—a southeastern coastal city of Australia with a large population

Adriatic Sea—an arm of the Mediterranean Sea that lies between Italy and the Balkan Peninsula

Aegean Sea—an arm of the Mediterranean Sea that lies off the eastern coast of Greece and the western coast of Turkey

Alaska Range—a U.S. mountain range in southern Alaska

Alexander Island—an island off of the Antarctic Peninsula

Algeria—one of the five nations of North Africa

Alpine nations—the very mountainous countries of Western Europe; includes the nations of Austria, Switzerland, and Liechtenstein

Alps—a tall, rugged mountain range that runs through much of south-central Europe

Altai Mountains—a mountain range that separates China from Central Asia

Amazon River—the largest river system in South America, flowing mostly through Brazil

Anatolian Plateau—a plateau in the Middle East that forms most of western Turkey

Andes Mountains—a mountain range that stretches along the full length of western South America

Angolan Plateau—a plateau area in Africa that stretches from southern Congo into Zambia and Angola

Antarctic Circle—an imaginary circle in Antarctica parallel to the equator

Antarctic Ocean—the stormy ocean that surrounds Antarctica; also known as the Southern Ocean

Antarctic Peninsula—a peninsula in northwestern Antarctica that extends toward South America

Antarctica—the continent at the extreme southern end of Earth

Apennines—a mountain range that runs down much of the length of Italy, in Western Europe

Appalachian Mountains—a mountain system in eastern North America, extending from northern Georgia to Maine in the United States and on into Quebec in Canada

Arabian Peninsula—the largest peninsula of the Middle East, jutting out into the Arabian Sea

Arabian Sea—an arm of the Indian Ocean lying between Arabia and India

Aral Sea—an inland sea in Central Asia between Uzbekistan and Kazakhstan

Arctic Ocean—the ocean that surrounds the North Pole, north of the Arctic Circle

Armenia—one of the eight nations of Central Asia

Asian Russia—the portion of Russia that is in Asia, east of the Ural Mountains

Atlantic seaboard—the urbanized area along the U.S. Atlantic coast

Atlas Mountains—a mountain system in North Africa that borders Morocco, Algeria, and Tunisia

Australia—an island continent lying between the Indian Ocean and the South Pacific Ocean

Australian Alps—mountains that contain Australia's highest elevations, located in the Great Dividing Range

Australian Capital Territory—a territory of Australia where the capital of Canberra is located

Ayers Rock—a massive rock formation that rises abruptly from the flat central portion of Australia's Western Plateau; also known as Uluru

Azerbaijan—one of the eight nations of Central Asia

Bahrain—an archipelago in the Middle East off the eastern coast of Saudi Arabia

Balkan Mountains—a mountain range that reaches west to east across central Bulgaria, in Eastern Europe

Balkan Peninsula—the largest peninsula in Eastern Europe; it juts into the Mediterranean Sea

Baltic Sea—a sea in northern Europe, an arm of the Atlantic Ocean, lying east of the Scandinavian Peninsula and west of the Baltic states

Baltic states—the three nations of Eastern Europe that border the Baltic Sea; includes Estonia, Latvia, and Lithuania

Bass Strait—the body of water between Australia and Tasmania

Bay of Bengal—an inlet of the Indian Ocean to the east of India

Beardmore Glacier—a glacier in West Antarctica

Beijing—the capital of China, in East Asia

Bering Strait—a narrow channel of water off the coast of Alaska connecting the Arctic Ocean and the Bering Sea, and separating North America and Asia

Black Sea—a sea between southeastern Europe and Asia, almost completely surrounded by land

Blue Nile—a tributary of the Nile River in Africa that starts in Ethiopia and flows northwest into the Nile

Bosporus—a narrow strait that connects the Black Sea with the Aegean Sea

Brahmaputra River—a river of the Indian Subcontinent that flows through Bangladesh

Brazilian Highlands—mountains of southeastern Brazil, in South America

Brisbane—an eastern coastal city of Australia with a large population

British Isles—the countries (Ireland and the United Kingdom) on islands located between the North Sea and the Atlantic Ocean

Brooks Range—the portion of the Rocky Mountain system that is in Alaska

Bucharest—the capital of Romania, an East European center of industry

Cairo—the capital of Egypt, in northeast Africa

Canadian Prairie—the fertile grasslands of central Canada

Canadian Rockies—the portion of the Rocky Mountain system that is in Canada

Canadian Shield—a large band of rocky highlands and plateaus in northern and eastern Canada

Canberra—the capital of Australia, in the southeastern part of the continent

Cape of Good Hope—a cape on the southern tip of Africa that juts out into the Atlantic Ocean

Cape York Peninsula—a large peninsula in northeastern Australia, between the Gulf of Carpentaria and the Coral Sea

Caribbean Sea—part of the Atlantic Ocean, bounded by the West Indies, Central America, and the northern coast of South America

Carpathian Mountains—a mountain system in Central Europe, stretching southeast through Slovakia, Poland, Ukraine and Romania

Cascade Range—a U.S. mountain range in Oregon and Washington

Caspian Sea—an inland sea that forms a natural boundary between Russia and many of its Central Asian neighbors

Caucasus Mountains—a mountain range that runs along the border between Russia and the Central Asian nations of Georgia and Azerbaijan

Celebes Sea—a part of the Pacific Ocean in East Asia, south of the Philippines

Central America—the extreme southern part of the North American continent

Central Lowlands—a mostly low, flat, dry region of Australia stretching to the west of the eastern mountain ranges

Central Plains—the fertile grasslands of the U.S. Midwest

Central Siberian Plateau—a rugged plateau region of central Siberia, in northern Asia

Chang River—China's longest navigable river, flowing from eastern China to the East China Sea

China—the largest nation in East Asia

Coast Mountains—a mountain range in western Canada and southern Alaska

Communism Peak—the highest mountain in Russia and Central Asia, located in the Tian Shan Mountains; also known as Ismail Samani Peak

Congo River—the second-longest river in Africa, flowing mostly through Democratic Republic of the Congo and Republic of the Congo and emptying into the Atlantic Ocean

Congo River basin—a lowland area of Africa near the equator that contains great tropical rain forests

Coral Sea—a part of the Pacific Ocean that lies off Australia's northeast coast

Corsica—a French island in the Mediterranean Sea, west of Italy

Crete—a Greek island located in the eastern Mediterranean Sea

Cyclades—a group of about 220 Greek islands in the Aegean Sea

Cyprus—the third-largest island in the Mediterranean Sea, lying off Turkey and Syria

Danube River—a long river in southern Europe, flowing from southern Germany eastward into the Black Sea

Darling River—a river in southeast Australia; the continent's longest, but sometimes dry, river

Deccan Plateau—a tableland that covers much of the Indian Peninsula, including about half of India; located between the Eastern and Western Ghat mountains

Deception Island—an island off of the Antarctic Peninsula

Dnieper River—one of the three longest rivers in European Russia

Don River—one of the three longest rivers in European Russia

Drakensberg Mountains—a mountain range that stretches along the southeastern coast of South Africa

East (Greater) Antarctica—the part of Antarctica that is to the east of the Transantarctic Mountains

East China Sea—a part of the Pacific Ocean east of China and west of Japan

Eastern Europe—the eastern portion of Europe, including the area that was formerly part of the Soviet bloc

Eastern Ghats—a mountain range that runs along India's coastline with the Bay of Bengal

Eastern Highlands—a series of high plateaus in eastern Australia

Egypt—one of the five nations of North Africa

Elburz Mountains—a mountain range of Iran, in the Middle East

Ellsworth Mountains—a mountain range that crosses West Antarctica

English Channel—a strait that connects the Atlantic Ocean to the North Sea and separates the British Isles and France

Ethiopian Highlands—an area of plateaus in western Ethiopia, in Africa

Euboea—one of the largest Greek islands, located in the Aegean Sea

Euphrates River—a river in the Middle East that flows from Turkey to Iraq and then joins with the Tigris River

European Russia—the portion of Russia that is in Europe, west of the Ural Mountains

Filchner Ice Shelf—an ice shelf in Antarctica that borders the Weddell Sea

Galápagos Islands—an island group in the Pacific Ocean west of Ecuador, to which they belong

Ganges River—a river of the Indian Subcontinent that flows through India into the Bay of Bengal

Georgia—one of the eight nations of Central Asia

Gibson Desert—a stony desert in the middle part of Australia's Western Plateau

Gobi Desert—a desert of East Asia that stretches across China and Mongolia

Great Australian Bight—a wide bay that indents Australia's southern coast

Great Barrier Reef—the world's largest coral reef, stretching along the northeastern coast of Australia, in the Coral Sea

Great Dividing Range—a series of mountain ranges running along the east coast of Australia

Great Indian Desert—a desert in northwest India and eastern Pakistan; also known as the Thar Desert

Great Lakes—five lakes (Erie, Huron, Michigan, Ontario, and Superior) at the border between the United States and Canada

Great Lakes region—a center of heavy industry in the United States and Canada, located around the Great Lakes

Great Plains—the fertile grasslands of the west-central United States

Great Rift Valley—a large sunken area of land that stretches from southwestern Asia down East Africa to Mozambique

Great Sandy Desert—a desert in the northern part of Australia's Western Plateau

Great Victorian Desert—a desert in the southern part of Australia's Western Plateau

Greece—a country on the largest peninsula in Eastern Europe, which juts out into the Mediterranean

Guangzhou—a Chinese city located on the mouth of the Xi River; also known as Canton

Guiana Highlands—a mountain range in northern South America

Gulf of Carpentaria—a gulf that indents the northern coast of Australia

Gulf of Guinea—a part of the Atlantic Ocean, off the west coast of Africa

Gulf of Mexico—an arm of the Atlantic Ocean, east of Mexico and south of the United States

Hawaii—a Pacific Ocean island group that is both part of Polynesia and a state of the United States

Himalayas—a very high mountain system that forms an arc along the border between the Indian Subcontinent and China

Hindu Kush—a mountain range of Afghanistan, in South Asia

Honshu—Japan's largest and most important island, in East Asia

Huang River—a river of East Asia that flows from eastern China to the Yellow Sea

Hudson Bay—an inland sea and arm of the Atlantic Ocean in northeastern Canada

Iberian Peninsula—a large peninsula in Western Europe that lies between the Mediterranean Sea and the Atlantic Ocean; it includes Spain and Portugal

Iceland—an island nation in the North Atlantic Ocean

Indian Ocean—an ocean south of Asia, between Africa and Australia

Indian Peninsula—a peninsula that juts out from South Asia into the Indian Ocean

Indian Subcontinent—the portion of southern Asia that includes India and its smaller neighbors

Indochina Peninsula—a peninsula of Southeast Asia that juts out from southeastern China into the South China Sea

Indonesia—an archipelago nation of East Asia consisting of many islands

Indus River—a river of the Indian Subcontinent that flows through Pakistan

Ionian islands—a group of Greek islands in the Ionian Sea

Ionian Sea—a section of the Mediterranean Sea that lies off the western coast of Greece

Irkutsk—an industrial city of Siberia, in northern Asia

Irrawaddy River—a river of South Asia that flows through Myanmar (Burma) and empties into the Bay of Bengal

Ismail Samani Peak—the highest mountain in Russia and Central Asia, located in the Tian Shan Mountains; also known as Communism Peak

Italian Peninsula—a large peninsula of Western Europe that extends into the Mediterranean Sea; it includes Italy, Vatican City, and San Marino

Japan—an archipelago nation of East Asia, located east of China across the Sea of Japan

Java Sea—a part of the Pacific Ocean between the Indonesian islands of Java and Borneo

Jordan River—a river in the Middle East that starts in Syria and flows south

Kabul River—a river of the Indian Subcontinent that flows through Afghanistan

Kalahari Desert—a desert that stretches across south central Africa

Kamchatka Peninsula—a peninsula that juts out from northeastern Russia into the Pacific Ocean and the Sea of Okhotsk

Kara Kum Desert—a desert of Central Asia that covers part of Uzbekistan and most of Turkmenistan

Karakoram Range—an Asian mountain range that stretches across northern India, Pakistan, and China

Katanga Plateau—a plateau area in Africa that stretches from southern Congo into Zambia and Angola

Kazakhstan—one of the eight nations of Central Asia

Kiev—the capital of Ukraine, a major industrial center of Eastern Europe

K2—a mountain in the Karakoram range; the world's second-largest mountain

Kunlun Mountains—an Asian mountain range in southwestern China

Lake Chad—a lake in Africa's desert fringe region, bordered by Niger, Chad, Cameroon, and Nigeria

Lake Eyre—a large, shallow salt lake in South Australia; usually dry

Lake Malawi (Nyasa)—the fourth-longest lake in the world, located mostly in the East African nation of Malawi

Lake Tanganyika—the longest freshwater lake in the world, located in east-central Africa and bordering the Democratic Republic of the Congo, Burundi, Tanzania, and Zambia

Lake Victoria—Africa's largest lake, located in East Africa and bordering Kenya, Uganda, and Tanzania

Lake Volta—a large lake in Ghana, not far from the Atlantic Ocean in West Africa

Lambert Glacier—a glacier in East Antarctica

Lena River—one of the three major rivers of Russia's Siberia, emptying into the Arctic Ocean

Libya—one of the five nations of North Africa

Llanos—the grasslands region of Venezuela, in South America

Magnitogorsk—a Russian industrial center in the Ural Mountains

Malay Peninsula—a peninsula of South Asia that stretches south to Singapore

Maldives—an archipelago nation of South Asia, located southwest of Sri Lanka

Mauna Loa—the world's largest volcano, located in the Hawaiian islands in the Pacific Ocean

Mediterranean nations—the southernmost countries of Europe; includes Portugal, Spain, Monaco, Italy, San Marino, Vatican City, and Malta

Mediterranean Sea—a large sea surrounded by southern Europe, northern Africa, and western Asia

Mekong River—a river of South Asia that flows south from China through the Indochina Peninsula and empties into the South China Sea

Melanesia—islands of Oceania that lie north and east of Australia in the Pacific Ocean

Melbourne—the capital of the southeastern Australian state of Victoria

Mexico—a Latin American nation just south of the United States, with which it shares a border

Micronesia—islands of Oceania that lie north of Melanesia in the Pacific Ocean

Milford Sound—a fiord on the southwest coast of New Zealand's South Island

Minsk—the capital city of Belarus, an important urban and industrial center of Eastern Europe

Mississippi River—a river in the central United States, flowing from Minnesota south to the Gulf of Mexico

Mississippi River system—one of the largest navigable river systems in the world; located in the central United States

Mongolia—the second-largest country in East Asia, located just south of Russia and north of China

Mongolian Plateau—a high tableland of Mongolia, in East Asia

Morocco—one of the five nations of North Africa

Moscow—Russia's capital and largest city, located in European Russia

Mount Ararat—one of the highest mountains in the Middle East, located in Turkey

Mount Damavand—the highest mountain in the Middle East, located in Iran

Mount Erebus—a mountain on Ross Island in Antarctica that is the continent's largest (and active) volcano

Mount Everest—the highest mountain in the world, located in the Himilayas on the border of Nepal and Tibet

Mount Kenya—a volcanic mountain in Kenya, in East Africa

Mount Kilimanjaro—Africa's highest mountain, located in Tanzania, in East Africa

Mount Kosciusko—Australia's tallest peak, located in the Snowy Mountains in eastern Australia

Murray River—a river in southeast Australia; the longest river on the continent that flows all year

Namib Desert—a desert that runs along the west coast of Namibia, in southern Africa

New Guinea—an island nation of East Asia, located north of Australia; the second-largest island in the world

New South Wales—an eastern state of Australia

Niger River—a West African river that flows through Mali, Niger, and Nigeria and then empties into the Gulf of Guinea

Nile River—the world's longest river, flowing north in Africa from Sudan to Egypt and emptying into the Mediterranean Sea

North Africa—the northern part of Africa; it includes the nations of Morocco, Algeria, Tunisia, Libya, and Egypt

North European Plain (or Lowland)—the fertile plain that stretches across northern Europe

North Island—one of the two main islands of New Zealand

North Korea—a nation in East Asia just east of northern China

North Sea—an arm of the Atlantic Ocean, between the British Isles and the northern European mainland

Northern Territory—a north-central territory of Australia

Novosibirsk—an industrial city of Siberia, in northern Asia

Nullarbor Plain—a dry, flat, treeless plain that runs along the south edge of Australia's Western Plateau

Ob-Irtysh River—one of the three major rivers of Russia's Siberia, emptying into the Arctic Ocean

Odessa—a port on the Black Sea in southern Ukraine, a major industrial center of Eastern Europe

Orinoco River—a South American river flowing mostly through Venezuela

Pacific Coast Region—the urbanized area along the U.S. Pacific coast

Pampas—a vast grassy plain of Argentina, in South America

Panama Canal—a waterway for ships that runs through Panama, in Central America, connecting the Caribbean Sea (in the Atlantic Ocean) with the Pacific Ocean

Papua New Guinea—an independent country on the eastern half of the East Asian island of New Guinea

Paraná River—a river in southern South America flowing from southern Brazil, along Paraguay's border, then into the Río de la Plata in Argentina

Patagonian Plateau—the dry, grassy plateau region east of the Andes Mountains in South America, mostly in Argentina

Peloponnese Peninsula—a peninsula that forms the southern part of mainland Greece, in Eastern Europe

Persian Gulf—an arm of the Arabian Sea that lies between the Arabian Peninsula and Iran

Perth—a southwestern coastal city of Australia with a large population

Philippine Sea—part of the Pacific Ocean, lying off of the Philippines and Japan

Philippines—an archipelago nation of East Asia that includes 1,700 islands

Plains of Hindustan—the plains of northern India, in South Asia

Plateau of Iran—a plateau at the center of Iran, in the Middle East

Plateau of Tibet—a tableland of Tibet, in southwestern China

Polynesia—islands of Oceania in the central and southern Pacific Ocean

Prague—the capital of the Czech Republic, an East European center for business and industry

Pyrenees—a mountain range that forms the border between Spain and France, in Western Europe

Queensland—an eastern state of Australia

Red Sea—a sea that lies between Africa and the Arabian Peninsula, connected to the Mediterranean Sea by the Suez Canal

Riga—the capital of Latvia, an East European urban center

Río de la Plata—an estuary in southeastern South America formed by the Uruguay and Paraná rivers

Rio Grande—a river separating the United States and Mexico

Rockefeller Plateau—an ice plateau in West Antarctica

Rocky Mountains—a mountain system of the western United States and Canada

Ronne Ice Shelf—an ice shelf in Antarctica that borders the Weddell Sea

Ross Ice Shelf—an ice shelf in Antarctica that borders the Ross Sea

Ross Island—an island off of the Antarctic Peninsula

Ruhr Valley—a leading coal-mining and industrial area in west-central Germany, in Western Europe

Russia—an enormous country in Eastern Europe and northern Asia, stretching from the Baltic Sea to the Pacific Ocean

Sahara Desert—a huge desert of North Africa that stretches from the west coast all the way across the continent to the Nile River in the east

Sahel—a semidesert area of Africa just below the Sahara Desert

Sardinia—an Italian island in the Mediterranean Sea, south of Corsica

Sayan Mountains—a mountain system in Central Asia that forms part of a natural border between Asian Russia and South Asia

Scandinavia—the northernmost region of Western Europe; includes the nations of Denmark, Iceland, Norway, Sweden, and Finland

Sea of Japan—an arm of the Pacific Ocean between Japan and East Asia

Sea of Okhotsk—an arm of the Pacific Ocean, off the east coast of Russia's Siberia

Shanghai—China's largest city, located at the mouth of the Chang River

Siberia—a vast region of Asian Russia between the Ural Mountains in the west and the Pacific Ocean in the east

Sicily—an Italian island off the southern tip of Italy

Sierra Madre—mountains that run through Mexico and Central America

Sierra Nevada—a U.S. mountain range in eastern California

Simpson Desert—a barren desert in east-central Australia

Sinai Peninsula—a small peninsula of the Middle East that juts out from the much larger Arabian Peninsula

Singapore—an island nation of South Asia that lies just off the Malay Peninsula

Snowy Mountains—mountains that are part of the Great Dividing Range in eastern Australia

Somali Peninsula—a large peninsula on the northeastern coast of sub-Saharan Africa

South America—the fourth-largest continent in the world, located mostly in the Southern Hemisphere

South Australia—the south-central state of Australia

South China Sea—an arm of the Pacific Ocean lying southeast of Southeast Asia's mainland

South Island—one of the two main islands of New Zealand

South Korea—a nation in East Asia just east of northern China

South Orkney Islands—islands off of the Antarctic Peninsula

South Polar Plateau—a high plateau that covers most of East Antarctica's interior

South Pole—the location at the bottom of the earth where all longitude lines meet

South Shetland Islands—islands off of the Antarctic Peninsula

Southeast Asia—the part of South Asia that is southeast of the Indian Subcontinent

Southern Ocean—the stormy ocean that surrounds Antarctica; also known as the Antarctic Ocean

Sri Lanka—an island nation of South Asia located in the Indian Ocean south of India

St. Lawrence Seaway—a large inland waterway system shared by the United States and Canada, linking the Great Lakes with the Atlantic Ocean

St. Petersburg—Russia's second-largest city and leading port, located in European Russia

Strait of Gibraltar—a narrow channel of water that separates Spain, in Western Europe, from the continent of Africa and connects the Mediterranean Sea and the Atlantic Ocean

sub-Saharan Africa—the African countries to the south of the Sahara Desert

Suez Canal—a human-made waterway that connects the eastern end of the Mediterranean Sea to the Red Sea

Sutherland Falls—a high waterfall on New Zealand's South Island

Sydney—the capital of the southeastern Australian state of New South Wales

Taiwan—an island nation in East Asia located off the east coast of China

Tajikistan—one of the eight nations of Central Asia

Tashkent—the capital of Uzbekistan and an industrial center of Central Asia

Tasman Sea—the section of the Pacific Ocean between Australia and New Zealand

Tasmania—a southeastern island state of Australia

Thar Desert—a desert in northwest India and eastern Pakistan; also known as the Great Indian Desert

Tian Shan Mountains—a mountain range that forms a natural border between China and Central Asia

Tibesti Mountains—a mountainous area in Chad, in Africa's desert fringe region

Tibet—a region of southwestern China just north of Nepal and Bhutan

Tigris River—a river in the Middle East that flows from Turkey to Iraq and then joins the Euphrates River

Timor Sea—an arm of the Indian Ocean between northwest Australia and Indonesia

Torres Strait—the body of water between northeastern Australia and New Guinea

Transantarctic Mountains—mountains that cut across Antarctica from north to south, separating East and West Antarctica

Tunisia—one of the five nations of North Africa

Turkey—a country of the Middle East on a peninsula bounded by the Aegan and Mediterranean seas

Turkmenistan—one of the eight nations of Central Asia

Tyrrhenian Sea—a part of the Mediterranean Sea off the western coast of Italy

Uluru—a massive rock formation that rises abruptly from the flat central portion of Australia's Western Plateau; also known as Ayers Rock

Ural Mountains—a mountain system that forms a natural divide between Europe and Asia

Uzbekistan—one of the eight nations of Central Asia

Verkhoyansk Range—an Asian mountain range in eastern Siberia

Victoria—a southeastern state of Australia

Victoria Falls—a great waterfall of the Zambezi River in east-southern Africa

Vinson Massif—Antarctica's highest mountain, located in the Ellsworth Mountains of West Antarctica

Volga River—the longest river in Europe, flowing through European Russia

Weddell Sea—a sea that indents Antarctica's northwestern coast

West (Lesser) Antarctica—the part of Antarctica that is to the west of the Transantarctic Mountains

West Indies—a large group of islands in the Caribbean Sea

West Siberian Plain—a flat, treeless Asian plain in western and southern Siberia

Western Australia—the Australian state that covers the western third of the continent

Western Europe—the western portion of Europe, the area that was never part of the Soviet bloc

Western Ghats—a mountain range that runs along India's coastline with the Arabian Sea

Western Plateau—a plateau that makes up the western two thirds of Australia

White Nile—a tributary of the Nile River in Africa that flows north from Lake Victoria into the Nile River

Xi River—a river of southern China that empties into the South China Sea

Yablonovy Range—a mountain system in Central Asia that forms part of a natural border between Asian Russia and South Asia

Yellow Sea—an arm of the East China Sea, between China and Korea

Yenisey River—one of the three major rivers of Russia's Siberia, emptying into the Arctic Ocean

Yucatán Peninsula—a peninsula in southeastern Mexico that separates the Gulf of Mexico from the Caribbean Sea

Zagros Mountains—a mountain system of Iran, in the Middle East

Zambezi River—a river of southern Africa that flows eastward from Zambia and empties into the Mozambique Channel of the Indian Ocean

GLOSSARY

Aboriginals (a-bor-IJ-nulz) Australia's native people

agriculture (A-gri-kul-chur) farming; the raising of crops and farm animals

alluvial plain (uh-LOO-vee-ul PLAYN) very fertile land formed by mud and soil carried by rivers

altitude (AL-ti-tood) height of a location above sea level

Antarctic Treaty (ant-ARK-tik TREE-tee) an agreement among many nations on how to manage Antarctica

arable (AR-uh-bul) able to support crops

archipelago (ar-kuh-PEL-uh-goh) a group or chain of many islands

arm (ARM) a large inlet of a larger body of water

Atlantic Convergence (ut-LAN-tik kun-VER-junts) a band along which Antarctica's Southern Ocean mixes its cold polar water with the warmer waters of the Atlantic, Indian, and Pacific oceans; *convergence* means "coming together"

atoll (A-tohl) a ring-shaped island with coral reefs that surround a shallow area of salt water called a lagoon

autonomous region (uh-TAH-nuh-mus REE-jun) a region with the power to govern itself

bauxite (BOKS-yt) ore used in making aluminum

bay (BAY) a partly enclosed inlet of the sea

belt (BELT) a region that has one special crop

bight (BYT) a curved bay

blizzard (BLI-zurd) a severe snowstorm with cold temperatures and heavy drifting snow

calving (KAV-ing) the process of iceberg formation, when chunks of ice shelves and glaciers break away and float off

cape (KAYP) a pointed piece of land that juts into the sea

capital (KAP-uh-tul) a city in which a country's government is located

---

PRONUNCIATION KEY

CAPITAL LETTERS show the stressed syllables.

a	as in m**a**t	f	as in **f**it	o	as in c**o**t, f**a**ther	uh	as in **a**bout, tak**e**n, lem**o**n, penc**i**l
ay	as in d**ay**, s**ay**	g	as in **g**o	oh	as in g**o**, n**o**te		
ch	as in **ch**ew	i	as in s**i**t	oo	as in t**oo**	ur	as in t**er**m
e	as in b**e**d	j	as in **j**ob, **g**em	sh	as in **sh**y	y	as in l**i**ne, fl**y**
ee	as in **e**ven, **ea**sy, n**ee**d	k	as in **c**ool, **k**ey	th	as in **th**in	zh	as in vi**s**ion, mea**s**ure
		ng	as in runni**ng**	u	as in b**u**t, s**o**me		

carat (KAR-ut) a unit of measure for diamonds and other precious gems

cash crops (KASH KROPS) crops that are grown to be sold on the market

Central Asian republics (SEN-trul AY-zhun ri-PUB-liks) Armenia, Azerbaijan, Georgia, Kazakhstan, Kyrgyzstan, Tajikistan, Turkmenistan, and Uzbekistan

channel (CHAN-ul) a body of water that connects two larger bodies of water

climate (KLY-mit) the usual weather in any one part of the world

climate map (KLY-mit MAP) a map that shows weather patterns

coast (KOHST) the land next to a body of salt water

commercial farming (kuh-MUR-shul FARM-ing) agriculture that involves raising cash crops

Commonwealth of Independent States (KOM-un-welth UV in-di-PEN-dunt STAYTS) alliance of nations that were once part of the Soviet Union

compass rose (KUM-pus ROHZ) on a map, a circle that shows direction

continents (KON-tuh-nents) large landmasses; on Earth, include Africa, Antarctica, Asia, Australia, Europe, North America, and South America

copra (KOH-pruh) the dried meat of coconuts, used for making soaps and lotions

coral reef (KOR-ul REEF) mass made up of the stony skeletons of small ocean creatures called polyps

crop yield (KROP YEELD) the amount of crops harvested per acre of land

cyclone (SY-klohn) a vast storm with violent, rotating winds

deforestation (dee-fohr-uh-STAY-shun) the cutting down of a forest, leaving few, if any, trees

degrees (di-GREEZ) units for measuring the position of latitude and longitude

delta (DEL-tuh) a fertile, fan-shaped area near the mouth of a river; created by alluvial deposits

densely populated (DENS-lee PO-pyuh-layt-ud) having many people per square mile

dependency (di-PEN-dun-see) a land or territory governed to some degree by another country

---

PRONUNCIATION KEY

CAPITAL LETTERS show the stressed syllables.

a as in m**a**t	f as in **f**it	o as in c**o**t, f**a**ther	uh as in **a**bout, tak**e**n, lem**o**n, penc**i**l
ay as in d**ay**, s**ay**	g as in **g**o	oh as in g**o**, n**o**te	ur as in t**er**m
ch as in **ch**ew	i as in s**i**t	oo as in t**oo**	y as in l**i**ne, fl**y**
e as in b**e**d	j as in **j**ob, **g**em	sh as in **sh**y	zh as in vi**s**ion, mea**s**ure
ee as in **e**ven, **ea**sy, n**ee**d	k as in **c**ool, **k**ey	th as in **th**in	
	ng as in runni**ng**	u as in b**u**t, s**o**me	

desert fringe nations (DEZ-urt FRINJ NAY-shunz) those nations on the southern edge of the Sahara Desert

developing economy (di-VEL-up-ing i-KAH-nuh-mee) an economy that does not yet have much industry

drought (DROWT) a long period of time with little or no rain

dry valley (DRY VA-lee) a rocky and ice-free valley in Antarctica's Transantarctic Mountains

due (DOO) when used with north, south, west, or east, it means "exactly"

East Coast (EEST KOHST) the land in the United States and Canada that is next to the Atlantic Ocean

elevation (EL-uh-vay-shun) the height above sea level

elevation map (EL-uh-vay-shun MAP) a map that shows how high the land is

embargo (em-BAR-goh) a ban on trade in a particular product

equator (i-KWAY-tur) on a map, a line running horizontally across the middle of the globe

erosion (i-ROH-zhun) the carrying away of topsoil by wind and rain

estuary (ES-chuh-wer-ee) a river or part of a river that is close to and mixes with the sea

euro (YUR-oh) currency used in most countries of the European Union (EU)

European Union (EU) (YUR-uh-pee-un YOON-yun) an organization of European countries that sets policies on matters of joint interest to its members

export (eks-PORT) to sell to other countries

fault (FAWLT) a break in Earth's crust where movement has taken place

Fertile Crescent (FUR-tul KRES-unt) a semicircle of fertile land in the Middle East

Fertile Triangle (FUR-tul TRY-ang-gul) a triangle-shaped area north of the Black Sea where most of Russia's crops are grown

fiord (fee-ORD) a narrow arm or inlet of the sea bordered by steep cliffs

fodder (FO-dur) food fed to livestock when grazing is not possible

PRONUNCIATION KEY

CAPITAL LETTERS show the stressed syllables.

a	as in m**a**t	f	as in **f**it	o	as in c**o**t, f**a**ther	uh	as in **a**bout, tak**e**n, lem**o**n, penc**i**l
ay	as in d**ay**, s**ay**	g	as in **g**o	oh	as in g**o**, n**o**te	ur	as in t**er**m
ch	as in **ch**ew	i	as in s**i**t	oo	as in t**oo**	y	as in l**i**ne, fl**y**
e	as in b**e**d	j	as in **j**ob, **g**em	sh	as in **sh**y	zh	as in vi**s**ion, mea**s**ure
ee	as in **e**ven, **ea**sy, n**ee**d	k	as in **c**ool, **k**ey	th	as in **th**in		
		ng	as in runni**ng**	u	as in b**u**t, s**o**me		

foothills (FUT-hilz) hilly region at the base of a mountain range

glacier (GLAY-shur) a riverlike mass of packed ice and snow that flows downward very slowly

globe (GLOHB) a three-dimensional map that is shaped like a ball

gulf (GULF) a large area of the sea that is partly enclosed by land

gum arabic (GUM AR-uh-bik) the product of the acacia tree; it is used to make glue, candy, and medicines

hemisphere (HEM-is-feer) half of the globe; identified as the Northern, Southern, Western, and Eastern hemispheres

hemp (HEMP) a strong plant fiber

high islands (HY Y-lundz) the islands of Oceania formed by volcanoes and earthquakes; these islands have mountains and hills

highlands (HY-lundz) areas of high plateaus

humus (HYOO-mus) the end product of decaying vegetable matter; makes soil rich and productive

hydroelectric power (hy-droh-i-LEK-trik POW-ur) the use of water power to produce electricity

hydrographer (hy-DRO-gruh-fur) a scientist who studies bodies of water

ice floes (YS FLOHZ) large areas of pieces of floating sea ice

ice shelf (YS SHELF) a flat, floating slab of ice

iceberg (YS-burg) a huge, floating mass of ice; most of it is underwater

industrialized (in-DUS-tree-uh-lyzd) having many industries

industries (IN-dus-treez) businesses that make and sell products

inland waterways (in-LAND WO-tur-wayz) rivers on which boats can travel

inlet (IN-let) a break in the shoreline that lets in water from a large body of water

international date line (in-tur-NASH-un-ul DAYT LYN) an imaginary line that runs north and south through the Pacific Ocean, near 180 degrees longitude on a map; where the calendar day starts

irrigation (ir-uh-GAY-shun) the process of redirecting water to places without enough rainfall

---

PRONUNCIATION KEY

CAPITAL LETTERS show the stressed syllables.

a as in m**a**t	f as in **f**it	o as in c**o**t, f**a**ther	uh as in **a**bout, tak**e**n, lem**o**n, penc**i**l
ay as in d**ay**, s**ay**	g as in **g**o	oh as in g**o**, n**o**te	ur as in t**er**m
ch as in **ch**ew	i as in s**i**t	oo as in t**oo**	y as in l**i**ne, fl**y**
e as in b**e**d	j as in **j**ob, **g**em	sh as in **sh**y	zh as in vi**s**ion, mea**s**ure
ee as in **e**ven, **ea**sy, n**ee**d	k as in **c**ool, **k**ey	th as in **th**in	
	ng as in runni**ng**	u as in b**u**t, s**o**me	

island (Y-lund) a body of land that is completely surrounded by water

isthmus (IS-mus) a narrow strip of land that is connected to the mainland

jute (JOOT) a plant that produces fiber, which is used to make such things as burlap and rugs

key (KEE) a list of symbols used on a map; also called a legend

land use map (LAND YOOS MAP) a map that shows which crops are grown in different areas

landforms (LAND-formz) the physical features of the planet, such as islands, mountains, rivers, oceans, and continents

landforms map (LAND-formz MAP) a map that shows the physical features of an area

landlocked (LAND-lokt) having no way to get to the sea

Latin America (LA-tin uh-MER-uh-kuh) all the nations that extend south of Canada and the United States

latitudes (LAT-uh-toodz) horizontal lines on a map or globe; also called parallels; known as the northern and southern latitudes

legend (LEJ-und) a list of symbols used on a map; also called a key

longitudes (LON-juh-toods) vertical lines on a map or globe; also called meridians

low islands (LOH Y-lundz) the islands of Oceania formed by coral reefs; these islands rise very little above sea level

maps (MAPS) flat pictures of Earth

meridians (muh-RID-ee-uns) vertical lines on a map or globe; also called longitudes

Middle East (MID-ul EEST) a group of countries west of South Asia that share elements of history, politics, and culture; the specific nations included change over time

mining (MYN-ing) the drawing out of mineral resources from beneath Earth's surface

monsoons (mon-SOONZ) winds in South Asia that are dry in winter and wet in summer

natural resources (NA-chuh-rul REE-sorsz) useful substances that are found in nature

navigable (NA-vi-guh-bul) able to be traveled on by boat

PRONUNCIATION KEY

CAPITAL LETTERS show the stressed syllables.

a	as in m**a**t	f	as in **f**it	o	as in c**o**t, f**a**ther	uh	as in **a**bout, tak**e**n, lem**o**n, penc**i**l
ay	as in d**ay**, s**ay**	g	as in **g**o	oh	as in g**o**, n**o**te		
ch	as in **ch**ew	i	as in s**i**t	oo	as in t**oo**	ur	as in t**er**m
e	as in b**e**d	j	as in **j**ob, **g**em	sh	as in **sh**y	y	as in l**i**ne, fl**y**
ee	as in **e**ven, **ea**sy, n**ee**d	k	as in **c**ool, **k**ey	th	as in **th**in	zh	as in vi**s**ion, mea**s**ure
		ng	as in runni**ng**	u	as in b**u**t, s**o**me		

Nile River basin (NYL RIV-ur BAY-sin) a fertile area of the long Nile River; extends north from East Africa through Egypt; where many of Egypt's agricultural and population centers are located

oases (oh-AY-seez) areas in deserts that are fed by underground water reserves

oceans (OH-shunz) large bodies of salt water; on Earth, include the Atlantic, Pacific, Indian, Arctic, and Southern oceans

ocean current (OH-shun KUR-unt) a movement of water that always flows in the same direction

Oceania (oh-shee-A-nee-uh) a name for the many groups of thousands of islands in the Pacific Ocean

oil refining (OYL ri-FYN-ing) the process of separating oil so it can be made into other, useful products

pack ice (PAK YS) dense clusters of frozen and pushed-together pieces of floating sea ice

parallels (PAR-uh-lelz) horizontal lines on a map or globe; also called latitudes

peninsula (puh-NIN-suh-luh) a piece of land that juts into the water

permafrost (PUR-muh-frost) soil that stays frozen all year round

plains (PLAYNZ) large areas of flat or nearly flat land

plantations (plan-TAY-shunz) large farms

plateaus (pla-TOHZ) flatlands that are higher than the land around them

polar desert (POH-lur DEZ-urt) a very cold and very dry area

political divisions (puh-LI-ti-kul di-VIZH-unz) geographic and governmental sections of a nation

population (po-pyuh-LAY-shun) a group of people living in one place

population density (po-pyuh-LAY-shun DEN-si-tee) the average number of people per square mile

population map (po-pyuh-LAY-shun MAP) a map that shows the population density of different areas

port (PORT) a city with a place where ships can dock

prairie (PRER-ee) a grassland with few or no trees

precipitation (pri-si-puh-TAY-shun) falling snow or rain

PRONUNCIATION KEY

CAPITAL LETTERS show the stressed syllables.

a	as in m**a**t	f	as in **f**it	o	as in c**o**t, f**a**ther	uh	as in **a**bout, tak**e**n, lem**o**n, penc**i**l
ay	as in d**ay**, s**ay**	g	as in **g**o	oh	as in g**o**, n**o**te	ur	as in t**er**m
ch	as in **ch**ew	i	as in s**i**t	oo	as in t**oo**	y	as in l**i**ne, fl**y**
e	as in b**e**d	j	as in **j**ob, **g**em	sh	as in **sh**y	zh	as in vi**si**on, mea**su**re
ee	as in **e**ven, **ea**sy, n**ee**d	k	as in **c**ool, **k**ey	th	as in **th**in		
		ng	as in runni**ng**	u	as in b**u**t, s**o**me		

prevailing wind (pri-VAYL-ing WIND) a wind that frequently blows from the same direction over an area

prime meridian (PRYM muh-RID-ee-un) a line between the Eastern and Western hemispheres; zero degrees longitude on a map

product map (PRO-dukt MAP) a map that shows what products are manufactured in different areas

productivity (proh-duk-TI-vuh-tee) in agriculture, how many crops the land produces

province (PRO-vints) the main political division of Canada

puna (POO-nuh) land at or above the tree line (up to 14,000 feet) in Latin America

rain forest (RAYN FOR-ist) a thick, evergreen forest that is wet most of the year

rainfall map (RAYN-fol MAP) a map that shows how much rain falls in different areas

ranges (RAYNJ-ez) rows of mountains that may extend for many miles

region (REE-jun) an area that shares one or more features

reservoir (RE-suh-vwor) a lake or pond in which water is collected and stored for use

resources map (REE-sorsz MAP) a map that shows where natural resources are located

road map (ROHD MAP) a map that shows where highways, roads, and bridges are located

Russian Federation (RUH-shin fed-uh-RAY-shun) the official name of Russia

Sahel (SA-hil) in Africa, the region between the Sahara Desert and the rest of sub-Saharan Africa; a semiarid region that includes Mauritania, Mali, Burkina Faso, Niger, and Chad

sand dunes (SAND DOONZ) mounds or ridges of sand found in sandy deserts

savanna (suh-VA-nuh) grasslands

scale (SKAYL) a rulerlike symbol on a map, used to measure distance

seas (SEEZ) smaller divisions of oceans, usually partly enclosed by land

sea ice (SEE YS) the frozen surface layer of ocean ice

sea level (SEE LEV-ul) the level of the surface of the ocean

PRONUNCIATION KEY

CAPITAL LETTERS show the stressed syllables.

a	as in m**a**t	f	as in **f**it	o	as in c**o**t, f**a**ther	uh	as in **a**bout, tak**e**n, lem**o**n, penc**i**l
ay	as in d**ay**, s**ay**	g	as in **g**o	oh	as in g**o**, n**o**te	ur	as in t**er**m
ch	as in **ch**ew	i	as in s**i**t	oo	as in t**oo**	y	as in l**i**ne, fl**y**
e	as in b**e**d	j	as in **j**ob, **g**em	sh	as in **sh**y	zh	as in vi**s**ion, mea**s**ure
ee	as in **e**ven, **ea**sy, n**ee**d	k	as in **c**ool, **k**ey	th	as in **th**in		
		ng	as in runni**ng**	u	as in b**u**t, s**o**me		

self-sufficient (SELF-suh-FISH-unt) as applied to agriculture, able to produce all the food that a country needs

semiarid (se-mee-AR-ud) a climate in which there is only enough rainfall to keep the area from becoming a desert

silt (SILT) rich soil carried by moving water

south magnetic pole (SOWTH mag-NE-tik POHL) the location where south magnetic forces are strongest

Soviet bloc (SOH-vee-ut BLOK) a group of countries whose governments, economies, and social organizations were dominated by the Soviet Union from 1948 to between 1989 and 1991

Soviet Union (SOH-vee-ut YOON-yun) The Union of Soviet Socialist Republics; a group of 15 countries dominated by Russia that dissolved in 1991; also called U.S.S.R.

sphere (SFEER) a solid round object, such as a globe

staple (STAY-pul) a crop that is produced widely and in large quantities

state (STAYT) the main political division of the United States

steppe (STEP) a treeless plain that may be semi-desert or covered with short grass

strait (STRAYT) a narrow channel of water that connects two larger bodies of water

subarctic (sub-ARK-tik) a cold climate in which the ground is not frozen all year; used to describe lands just outside the Arctic Circle; also called cold forest

subcontinent (sub-KON-tuh-nent) a large part of a larger landmass that is somewhat separate from it

sub-Saharan Africa (sub-suh-HAR-un A-fri-kuh) the part of Africa that lies below the Sahara Desert

subsistence farming (sub-SIS-tuns FARM-ing) agriculture that involves growing just enough food for the farm family's needs, not for sale

tableland (TAY-buhl-land) a plateau that drops off suddenly, as a table does

taiga (TY-guh) a forest found in northern latitudes

temperate (TEM-pur-it) neither extremely hot nor extremely cold

terracing (TER-us-ing) an agricultural system in which farmers cut step-like level areas into the sides of hills

---

PRONUNCIATION KEY

CAPITAL LETTERS show the stressed syllables.

a	as in m**a**t	f	as in **f**it	o	as in c**o**t, f**a**ther	uh	as in **a**bout, tak**e**n, lem**o**n, penc**i**l
ay	as in d**ay**, s**ay**	g	as in **g**o	oh	as in g**o**, n**o**te	ur	as in t**er**m
ch	as in **ch**ew	i	as in s**i**t	oo	as in t**oo**	y	as in l**i**ne, fl**y**
e	as in b**e**d	j	as in **j**ob, **g**em	sh	as in **sh**y	zh	as in vi**s**ion, mea**s**ure
ee	as in **e**ven, **ea**sy, n**ee**d	k	as in **c**ool, **k**ey	th	as in **th**in		
		ng	as in runni**ng**	u	as in b**u**t, s**o**me		

terrain (tuh-RAYN) land, especially its physical features

textiles (TEKS-tylz) materials used for clothing and other soft goods

38th parallel (THUR-tee-AYTH PAR-uh-lel) the latitude that is the dividing line between North Korea and South Korea

tierra caliente (tee-ER-uh cal-ee-EN-tay) hot land

tierra fría (tee-ER-uh FREE-uh) cold land

tierra templada (tee-ER-uh tem-PLAH-duh) temperate land

Tigris-Euphrates system (TI-grus-yuh-FRAY-teez SIS-tuhm) the combined river basin of the Tigris and Euphrates rivers where many agricultural and population centers are located

tin (TIN) metal used in many products, such as food containers

Trans-Siberian Railroad (TRANS-si-BIR-ee-un RAYL-rohd) the longest railroad line in the world; stretches from St. Petersburg on the Baltic Sea to Vladivostok on the Sea of Japan

trench (TRENCH) a long, deep valley formed when there is land movement

tributaries (TRIB-yuh-ter-eez) the branches of a major river

tropics (TROP-iks) the very warm area near the equator; extends north to the Tropic of Cancer and south to the Tropic of Capricorn

tsunami (soo-NO-mee/tsoo-NO-mee) a huge ocean wave caused by a volcanic eruption or an undersea earthquake

tundra (TUN-druh) vast, level, treeless plains of the Arctic region

typhoon (ty-FOON) a severe tropical storm with strong winds and heavy rains

unpredictable rainfall (un-pri-DIK-tuh-bul RAYN-fol) rainfall that cannot be predicted because it may come too often or too heavily, or may not fall often enough or in great enough amounts

urban (UR-bun) having to do with a city or city life

volcanic (vol-KA-nik) formed when volcanoes erupted

volcano (vol-KAY-noh) a vent in Earth's crust that can throw out molten (melted) rock, rock pieces, gases, and ash

---

PRONUNCIATION KEY

CAPITAL LETTERS show the stressed syllables.

a	as in m**a**t	f	as in **f**it	o	as in c**o**t, f**a**ther	uh	as in **a**bout, tak**e**n, lem**o**n, penc**i**l
ay	as in d**ay**, s**ay**	g	as in **g**o	oh	as in g**o**, n**o**te	ur	as in t**er**m
ch	as in **ch**ew	i	as in s**i**t	oo	as in t**oo**	y	as in l**i**ne, fl**y**
e	as in b**e**d	j	as in **j**ob, **g**em	sh	as in **sh**y	zh	as in vi**si**on, mea**s**ure
ee	as in **e**ven, **ea**sy, n**ee**d	k	as in **c**ool, **k**ey	th	as in **th**in		
		ng	as in runni**ng**	u	as in b**u**t, s**o**me		

warm westerlies (WOHRM WES-tur-leez) winds that blow west to east over warm currents in the Atlantic Ocean; winds that help make Western Europe's climate mild

waterway (WO-tur-way) a body of water that is navigable

West Coast (WEST KOHST) the land in the United States and Canada that is next to the Pacific Ocean

PRONUNCIATION KEY

CAPITAL LETTERS show the stressed syllables.

a	as in m**a**t	f	as in **f**it	o	as in c**o**t, f**a**ther	uh	as in **a**bout, tak**e**n, l**e**m**o**n, penc**i**l
ay	as in d**ay**, s**ay**	g	as in **g**o	oh	as in g**o**, n**o**te	ur	as in t**er**m
ch	as in **ch**ew	i	as in s**i**t	oo	as in t**oo**	y	as in l**i**ne, fl**y**
e	as in b**e**d	j	as in **j**ob, **g**em	sh	as in **sh**y	zh	as in vi**si**on, mea**su**re
ee	as in **e**ven, **ea**sy, n**ee**d	k	as in **c**ool, **k**ey	th	as in **th**in		
		ng	as in runni**ng**	u	as in b**u**t, s**o**me		